Baron Henry Thring

Practical Legislation

The Composition and Language of Acts of Parliament

Baron Henry Thring

Practical Legislation
The Composition and Language of Acts of Parliament
ISBN/EAN: 9783337154813

Printed in Europe, USA, Canada, Australia, Japan

Cover: Foto ©Suzi / pixelio.de

More available books at **www.hansebooks.com**

PRACTICAL LEGISLATION;

OR,

THE COMPOSITION AND LANGUAGE

OF

ACTS OF PARLIAMENT,

BY

SIR HENRY THRING, K.C.B.,

THE PARLIAMENTARY COUNSEL.

LONDON:
Printed for Her Majesty's Stationery Office,

AND SOLD BY

CLOWES & SONS, Charing Cross; LONGMAN & Co., Paternoster Row;
TRÜBNER & Co., Ludgate Hill; KNIGHT & Co., 90, Fleet Street;
STEVENS & SONS, 119, Chancery Lane; and SHAW & SONS, Fetter Lane.

TABLE OF CONTENTS.

CHAPTER I.

Introductory Observations.

CHAPTER II.

Arrangement of Subject-Matter of an Act.

CHAPTER III.

Composition of Sentences.

Chapter IV.

General Observations.

APPENDIX I.

Part 1.

Part 2.

APPENDIX II.

PREFACE.

THIS work has been written as a practical guide for persons en- Object of work.
gaged in preparing Acts of Parliament. It is based on Instructions
to Draftsmen, which have for some years been in use in the
office of the Parliamentary Counsel. Hence its didactic tone and
its mention of various topics which would, if it were addressed to
adepts and not to learners, be excluded as trivial and well known,
but which are frequently neglected in practice. It is divided into Summary of
four parts. The first part instructs the draftsman as to the mode of contents of work.
getting up his subject. The second part deals with the arrange-
ment of the subject matter of an Act of Parliament, pointing out
the expediency of presenting the law to Parliament in a clear
and concise form, and insisting on the advantage of separating
principle from detail, and material from comparatively immaterial provisions. The third part is occupied with the subject of the
composition of sentences. The fourth part makes observations
and suggestions with respect to preambles, the commencement of
Acts, the construction of Acts, and other formal matters. Two
appendices follow, the first containing analyses of two selected
Acts, illustrative of the rules as to arrangement, the second giving
a number of forms adapted for ordinary use.

As no special reference is made to Consolidation or Codification, Absence of
it may be well to say in the preface a word on those subjects, and special instruc-
tions as to
to point out the applicability to them of the rules laid down in codification
and consolida-
this work. tion.

Codification is the reduction into a systematic form of the whole Meaning of
of the law relating to a given subject, that is to say, of the Common codification.
Law, the Case Law, and the Statute Law; while consolidation
differs from codification in this alone, that it omits the Common
Law and comprises only the Statute Law relating to a subject as
illustrated or explained by judicial decisions.

The writer has elsewhere explained the mode in which, according Summary of
to his judgment, codification or systematic consolidation should be processes
essential to
codification.

proceeded with.(*a*) Such a work must be gradual. 1st. The Common Law must be extracted from the authoritative text-books in which it is embedded, and so much as is not capable of being absorbed into the Statute Law must be digested into an Institute or Book of Maxims. 2nd. The Case Law must be reduced into a manageable bulk by publishing leading cases, (or cases which are in reality legislative decisions given by the judges,) and by setting aside in a Digest the effect of such cases as are merely illustrative of Statute Law or Common Law, and are not readily incorporated therein, or by issuing an expurgated edition of the older Reports. 3rd. The Statute Law must first be indexed, and then be consolidated in classified groups. When the above-mentioned processes have been completed, a code will be readily made by absorbing into the text of the classified groups of Statute Law any portion of the Common Law or Case Law left outside the Institute of Maxims.

Result of codification a series of Acts of Parliament. It is unnecessary to enter into further details to show that the codification or consolidation of a particular branch of law is merely another mode of expressing the composition of an Act or series of Acts, embodying in the case of codification the whole of that law, and in the case of consolidation a portion only.

Rules applicable to ordinary Acts of Parliament applicable to code. The extent of the subject matter, however, cannot affect the applicability of the rules of composition. Indeed, codification or consolidation is in many respects an easier task than the preparation of the amending Acts required for current legislation. Just as it is easier for an architect to build a house from its foundations than to convert an old inconvenient house into a modern convenient one, so a draftsman can more readily construct an Act dealing with the whole of the subject matter, than an Act in which the new law must be adjusted and made to harmonise with the old and often conflicting provisions of former Acts.

Slight qualification of rules as to arrangement in case of code. The only qualification to be made in the application of the rules laid down in this work to a code or a consolidating Act, relates to the arrangement of groups of sections, and is this, that in making the plan for the arrangement of the sections of a code or consolidating Act, Parliamentary considerations may usually be disregarded, and logical considerations, as they are called, be exclusively adhered to. This difference, however, is very slight,

(*a*.) "Simplification of the Law," reprinted by permission from the Quarterly Review of Jan. 7, 1874. London, Robert John Bush, 32, Charing Cross, S.W.

as in the great majority of cases the most scientific and logical arrangement is the one which is best for Parliamentary purposes.

It must be admitted that no rules are found in this treatise for the arrangement amongst themselves of *groups* of statutes, whether such statutes are codes or merely consolidating Acts ; in other words, no general outline of a code embracing the whole or a great part of the English law is laid down, or attempted to be laid down. This omission is designed, as any considerations *à priori* of the mutual relations of laws to each other, apart from convenience of administration, are too abstract to find a place in an elementary treatise, and may well wait for solution till the component parts of the code have been to a great extent completed. *Arrangement of code not treated of.*

To say the truth, promoters of codification would seem to be too much given to theoretical in preference to practical considerations.   They spend much labour in determining the proper arrangement of a code before they have attempted to draw an Act or series of Acts embodying even partially any one branch of the law intended to be included in such code. Yet if the statute book were once divided into a number of well-drawn Acts embodying both Statute and Common Law, all that would be required to make a code would be to group those Acts according to some convenient arrangement, probably according to the exigencies of the judicial or administrative departments of the Government. A good code is a collection of good Acts, in the same way as a good library is a collection of good books, or a good picture gallery a collection of good pictures. The exact arrangement of the several Acts in the code is of very little importance as compared with the excellence of the Acts themselves ; in the same way, to continue the comparison, as in the case of a library or picture gallery the character of the books or pictures, far more than their relative arrangement, determines the value of the whole collection. Moreover a good Index is in practice a not ineffectual cure for any defects in the arrangement of a code, a library, or a picture gallery. *Arrangement immaterial as compared with composition of Acts comprising code.*

Having thus deviated into questions of general legislation, it may be well to remark that the writer does not concur in the views of those critics who underrate English law, as compared with foreign codes, and object altogether to Parliamentary supervision of English legislation.   Uncouth although it may be in form, English law is just and specific in its directions to an extent *Excellence of English law in substance though uncouth in form.*

never yet attained by a foreign code; and leaves (and this is
the practical perfection of law) less to the discretion of the judge
than any other system of jurisprudence.

Possibility of improving form without injuring substance. The real problem is to attain the advantages of a systematic code without destroying the fulness of expression and copiousness of illustration which characterise English law; that such an attainment is possible by gradual steps the writer has endeavoured elsewhere to show, and he need not here repeat his views.

Observations on Parliamentary supervision. With respect to Parliamentary supervision, it is difficult to conceive a more searching scrutiny than an opposed Bill when in Committee receives at the hands of Parliament; to dispense with such a scrutiny in the case of new legislation would be most unadvisable. On the other hand, the evils of Parliamentary interference are no doubt seriously felt with respect to laws, the principles of which have been finally settled by the Legislature, and which it is desirable to codify or consolidate with a view to give symmetry to their form without alteration of their substance. To such a codification or consolidation the House of Commons too often creates insuperable obstacles by reviving old subjects of controversy, and by insisting on discussing settled principles. The duty of Parliament in such cases would seem to be to ascertain only that the new Bill correctly represents the old law. To effect this, all that is required would be to appoint in each House of Parliament a committee charged with the consideration of such Bills, and to have it understood that Bills once approved by such committees should pass without discussion.

It remains only to add that the writer has been assisted in the preparation of the forms contained in the Second Appendix, and generally in the work, by Mr. Jenkyns, the Assistant Parliamentary Counsel; Mr. C. P. Ilbert, Mr. G. A. R. Fitz Gerald, and other friends have also afforded great aid by suggestions and criticisms made during the progress of the work through the press.

The Index has been prepared by Mr. C. S. Maine.

Nov. 10, 1877.   HENRY THRING.

PRACTICAL LEGISLATION.

CHAPTER I.

INTRODUCTORY OBSERVATIONS.

WHEN instructions for an Act (*a*) are given to a draftsman, his first step should be to acquaint himself with the *whole* of the existing law relating to the subject-matter of the Act which he is directed to prepare.

This completeness of knowledge is essential, for so complex are the relations of the various parts of English law that however limited the scope of an Act apparently may be, yet the law with which it deals may chance to be an offshoot of some larger branch of jurisprudence, and the draftsman, by the alteration of a definition or the introduction of a superfluous provision, may unintentionally subvert a settled principle of common law or disturb a series of legislative enactments. Every Act in which a fine is imposed affords an example of what has been said. A number of Acts define the mode in which fines are to be enforced, and award a scale of imprisonment to be inflicted in default of their being paid. A draftsman ignorant of these Acts will almost certainly contravene their provisions by varying the process for enforcing the fines or altering the scale of imprisonment (*b*).

Complete knowledge of law essential.

If the draftsman approaches a subject for the first time, he will do well, as a first step, to endeavour to obtain a general view of its whole extent. This may be done by reading any modern treatise containing the law. The sooner, however, that he discards such a treatise, and has recourse to the original authorities, the more readily will his task be accomplished of arriving at an accurate knowledge of his subject.

Method of getting up law.

In getting up the statute law it is a convenient plan to obtain Queen's Printer's copies of the Acts required, and, tying them together, to read them through, beginning with the last Act, and so on up to the earliest, striking out the repealed provisions.

(*a*.) In this work the term " Act " will be used in place of " Bill," and " section " in place of " clause," though an Act while in the draftsman's hands is more correctly termed a Bill, and its sections " clauses."

(*b*.) See the Summary Jurisdiction Act, 11 & 12 Vict. c. 43. and the Amending Acts, also 28 & 29 Vict. c. 127. " The Small Penalties Act, 1865." This latter Act will probably be repealed by the Summary Jurisdiction Act of the session of 1878.

In studying the case law, the best method is to discover the leading case on a given point, and having thoroughly mastered the details, to pursue the law through all subsequent cases to the date of the last decision. A little practice, aided by an index of cases, will enable the student to complete his investigation very rapidly.

Cases readily range themselves into two classes, namely, those that lay down new principles, and those that merely illustrate the application of known rules. A reference to the marginal notes will generally suffice to give a sufficient knowledge of an illustrative case, while a case laying down a new principle of law is, to the extent to which the principle is new, a leading case, and must be thoroughly mastered in detail.

This distinction between leading cases and illustrative cases is most important in reference to legislation. Leading cases constitute in effect judicial legislation, and admit of being codified by having their principles expressed in a legislative form. Illustrative cases are merely explanations or illustrations of the law, and may either be dismissed altogether by the draftsman, or have their influence on legislation expressed by the insertion of a few words in a section to remove a doubt or explain a difficulty.

Take, as examples of the difference between cases laying down new principles of law or judicial enactments and merely illustrative cases, two decisions in relation to bills of exchange.

The negotiability of a bill of exchange was determined by a judicial decision. This decision, being followed, soon passed into the domain of settled law, and, when thus established, amounted to an enactment that bills of exchange are negotiable.

The decision in the case of *Rees* v. *Warwick*, 2 B. & Ald. 113, on the question whether a letter from the drawee to the drawer, stating "your bill 100*l.* shall have attention" amounts to an acceptance, involves no principle or general proposition of law, but is merely an illustration of the law in a particular case.

If the subject matter of a proposed Act be very extensive, the general case law must be studied in a text book, and the method recommended of going back to a leading case and tracing the law downwards must be reserved for such points as from their difficulty or importance deserve to be set aside for special investigation.

In studying the common law, the earlier authorities, as for example, Coke upon Littleton and Hawkins' Pleas of the Crown, should be consulted in preference to more modern books. The common law having thus been traced to its origin, the later treatises may be looked at for the purpose of ascertaining, in a compendious manner, the numerous changes introduced by statute in almost every department of that law.

Whatever method of studying law be adopted, the draftsman should as far as possible trust to his memory for collecting the results, making notes very seldom, and those extremely concise, in the nature of an index indicating where important propositions of law are to be found rather than in the form of extracts from or a statement of the law itself. By adopting this plan he will acquire a habit of carrying in his mind a long and complicated set of provisions for a time sufficient to pass the whole in review, and thus ascertain the true relation which the various parts bear to each other, a process essential to the completion of a clear and well-arranged scheme of legislation.

Where any considerable alteration of the law is to be effected, the draftsman will do well to keep a record of the law which he has acquired, and of the changes introduced by the Act which he is preparing, by writing a memorandum containing in concise terms the history of the law which he has been studying, and pointing out the principal points in which his Act proposes to alter the existing law, adducing, shortly, the reasons for the alterations made.

Before concluding this chapter, it will be convenient to explain the sense in which the expressions "Act of Parliament" and "enactment" are used in this work, and to point out the meaning of a division which has been made of Acts of Parliament into simple and complex Acts.

2. Explanation of certain terms used in work. Act of Parliament.

An Act of Parliament may for the purpose of this work be considered as a series of declarations of the Legislature enforcing certain rules of conduct, or conferring certain rights upon or withholding them from certain persons or classes of persons.

This description of an Act of Parliament includes a principal Act with its various amending Acts, and this is intentional; for a series of Acts relating to the same subject is in fact, and ought for all purposes of arrangement to be treated as, a single Act of Parliament.

The separate declarations of the Legislature contained in an Act of Parliament will be called Enactments.

Enactments.

It is possible, of course, that an Act may contain only one enactment, and in that case there is no distinction between "Act of Parliament" and "enactment."

Acts are referred to as simple and complex Acts. An Act is simple when its principle can be declared in one enactment and the whole of the Act is employed in working out that principle.

Simple and complex Acts.

For example, the Stock Certificate Act, 1863, (26 & 27 Vict. c. 28.) is a simple Act, as the principle that a person may obtain a stock certificate is declared in a single enactment, while the remainder of the Act is occupied with showing how the principles declared in such enactment are to be worked out in detail.

24 & 25 Vict. c. 133. On the other hand, the Land Drainage Act, 1861, is a complex Act, as it deals in three parts with the following different legal heads, Part I.—The issue of Commissions of Sewers for new areas on recommendation of Inclosure Commissioners; Part II.—The constitution of elective drainage districts on the application of certain proprietors; and Part III.—The power of private owners to procure outfalls. Again:—The Irish Church Act, 1869, is a complex Act, as it consists (1) of the disestablishment, and (2) of the disendowment of the Church.

32 & 33 Vict. c. 42. The above terms make no pretensions to logical accuracy, but will be found convenient for describing certain species of enactments and certain descriptions of Acts which practically must be dealt with by the draftsman as requiring different modes of treatment.

CHAPTER II.

Arrangement of Subject-Matter of an Act.

3. Difficulty of Arrangement. Possessed of a full knowledge of his subject the draftsman will, if the Act be a long one, for example, an Irish Church Act (see the Irish Church Act, 1869, 32 & 33 Vict. c. 42.); an Irish Land Act (see the Landlord and Tenant (Ireland) Act, 1870, 33 & 34 Vict. c. 46.); a Bankruptcy Act (see The Bankruptcy Act, 1869, 32 & 33 Vict. c. 71.) (a); a Land Transfer Act (see The Land Transfer Act, 1875, 38 & 39 Vict. c. 87.); an Explosive Substances Act (see The Explosive Substances Act, 1875, 38 & 39 Vict. c. 17.), feel himself bewildered by the multiplicity of the enactments and the extent of his task.

4. Selection and Statement of Principles. His first step must be, in the case of a simple Act, to settle the principle or leading motive, and in the case of a complex Act the several principles or leading motives of the Act on which he is engaged.

With respect to the mode in which the principle is to be selected, and where there is more than one principle in the Act the arrangement of the principles, the draftsman will, where an Act is of political consequence, be guided by the express instructions of the minister. Before an Act of political importance is introduced, an able minister settles in his own mind the questions on which divisions are to be taken, and forms a general idea of the

(a.) Appendix II., Part I.

mode in which those questions should be presented to Parliament. He then instructs the draftsman to follow his directions in these respects, and to frame his Act in accordance with the leading questions to be submitted to Parliament.

In a simple Act, the principle when selected must be enunciated in its most concise form at the very outset of the Act either in one section or in two or more consecutive sections, as the subject may require. In a complex Act, the principles should be arranged in different parts of the Act, and each part of the Act should be treated as a simple Act, and contain its principle enunciated in the most concise form at the outset of the part. In short, the test of the arrangement of an Act or part as respects the principle, is this :—If the reader, after mastering the first two or three sections, comprehends the whole drift of the Act or of the part, the Act or part is in that respect well arranged. The Act or part is as regards principle ill-arranged in proportion as the principle is distributed throughout a number of sections, and broken up by conditions and provisions from which the reader has to extract it bit by bit.

This arrangement is to be recommended both for Parliamentary and for practical reasons. It enables Parliament to decide at once on the principle of an Act unembarrassed by the consideration of details, and it places before the reader at the outset a clear view of the law intended to be enacted, without the confusing intermixture of the conditions under which and the mode in which that law is to be administered. The principle thus being settled, the conditions can be considered separately, and no confusion arises between objections of principle and objections of detail.

The importance of selecting the principles and stating them in a concise form at the outset of an Act or division of an Act is so great that it will be illustrated by numerous examples, beginning with simple Acts and proceeding to complex Acts.

5. ILLUSTRATIONS OF SELECTION AND STATEMENT OF PRINCIPLES IN SIMPLE ACTS. 31 & 32 Vict. c. 109.

The simplest form of enactment is contained in one short clause. For example, the Compulsory Church Rate Abolition Act, 1868, provides in its first section as follows :—

" From and after the passing of this Act, no suit
" shall be instituted or proceeding taken in any eccle-
" siastical or other court, or before any justice or
" magistrate, to enforce or compel the payment of
" any church rate made in any parish or place in
" England or Wales."

The passing of that clause abolishes compulsory church rates, and the remainder of the Act is taken up with providing for voluntary church rates, and making the proper reservations for cases in which money had been lent on the security of rates.

39 & 40 Vict.
c. 77.

The Cruelty to Animals Act, 1876, relating to vivisection, expresses its intention by declaring—

"That a person shall not perform on a living animal any "experiment calculated to give pain, except subject to the restric-"tions imposed by the Act," and imposes a penalty on any person performing any experiment calculated to give pain, in contravention of the Act.

Under that section, all experiments on living animals calculated to give pain are primâ facie prohibited, and, as might be expected, the remainder of the Act is employed in declaring the conditions under which, in certain cases and for certain purposes, experiments may be performed on living animals.

16 & 17 Vict.
c. 51.

Perhaps the best illustration of the concentration of the principle of a whole Act into one clause is found in the Succession Duty Act, 1853, s. 2, which is as follows :—

"Every past or future disposition of property,
"by reason whereof any person has or shall become
"beneficially entitled to any property, or the income
"thereof, upon the death of any person dying after
"the time appointed for the commencement of this
"Act, either immediately or after any interval, either
"certainly or contingently, and either originally or
"by way of substitutive limitation, and every devo-
"lution by law of any beneficial interest in property,
"or the income thereof, upon the death of any person
"dying after the time appointed for the commence-
"ment of this Act, to any other person, in possession
"or expectancy, shall be deemed to have conferred
"or to confer on the person entitled by reason of any
"such disposition or devolution a "succession;" and
"the term "successor" shall denote the person so
"entitled; and the term "predecessor" shall denote
"the settlor, disponer, testator, obligor, ancestor, or
"other person from whom the interest of the suc-
"cessor is or shall be derived."

This section embraces not only the whole subject matter of succession duty, but that of the Legacy Duty Acts also, and the remainder of the Act is occupied in excepting successions subject to the Legacy Duty Acts and in illustrating particular examples of s. 2, or in making rules for carrying s. 2 into effect.*

25 & 26 Vict.
c. 89.
26 & 27 Vict.
c. 28.
37 & 38 Vict.
c. 67.
39 & 40 Vict.
c. xliii. (Local).

* *Note.*—See also the Companies Act, 1862, in which s. 6, the Stock Certificates Act, 1863, in which s. 3, and the Slaughter-houses, &c. (Metropolis) Act, 1874, in which ss. 2 and 3 enunciate the principle of the Act; also the Army Corps Training Act, 1876, in which s. 2 is the effective enactment.

A similar mode of arrangement is exemplified by complex Acts.

The Irish Church Act, 1869, provides for (1) the disestablishment, (2) the disendowment of thĕ Church. The disestablishment is enunciated in s. 2, which is as follows :—

> "On and after the first day of January one thousand eight hundred and seventy-one the said union created by Act of Parliament between the Churches of England and Ireland shall be dissolved, and the said Church of Ireland, herein-after referred to as 'the said Church' shall cease to be established by law."

Nothing further was required to complete that enactment. The disendowment and formation of a new Church body occupy the whole of the remainder of the Act. The principle of disendowment is enunciated in s. 11, which ought to have followed s. 2, without the interposition of the sections relating to the constitution of the Commissioners.

The Land Drainage Act, 1861, consists of the following heads, divided in the Act into separate parts :—Part I.—The issue of Commissions of Sewers for new areas on recommendation of Inclosure Commissioners. Part II.—The constitution of elective drainage districts on the application of certain proprietors. Part III.—The power of private owners to procure outfalls.

A reference to Part I. (s. 4.), to Part II. (ss. 63 & 64), and Part III. (s. 72) will illustrate the rule of enunciating in one section the principle of a part of an Act.

The Ballot Act, 1872, had two objects in view, the alteration of the law relating to the nomination of candidates at Parliamentary elections and the alteration of the law relating to the mode of voting. It was necessary to separate the essential conditions of the law from the detailed provisions intended to carry it into effect. Accordingly s. 1 lays down the rules for nomination, and s. 2 creates a secret ballot with all its necessary conditions; while the detailed provisions required to give effect to a secret ballot are contained in a schedule of 63 articles.

Before concluding these illustrations it may be well to call attention to a difference in the mode of expressing the principle of an Act in cases where the principle cannot be enunciated in one enactment (as in the example of section one of the Compulsory Church Rates Abolition Act), but must range over several enactments. Where several enactments are required, there are two modes of dealing with the matter. In the one, the principle may be enunciated by itself in an independent enactment, without any words connecting it with its

---

Marginal notes:

6. ILLUSTRATIONS OF SELECTION AND STATEMENT OF PRINCIPLES IN COMPLEX ACTS.
32 & 33 Vict. c. 42.

24 & 25 Vict. c. 133.

35 & 36 Vict. c. 33.

7. OBSERVATIONS AS TO MODE OF FRAMING PRINCIPAL AND SUBORDINATE ENACTMENTS.

subsequent subordinate enactments, or the principle may at the outset be linked on by connecting words to the whole or to any part of its subordinate enactments. Similarly, the subordinate enactments may be expressed in words wholly unconnected with each other, or may be partially connected by words referring from one enactment to the other.

39 & 40 Vict. c. 59.
As an illustration of the first mode of dealing, take the Appellate Jurisdiction Act, 1876. That Act declares, in four separate and unconnected sections (1) the cases in which an appeal lies to the House of Lords; (2) the form of appeal to the House of Lords ; (3) the attendance of a certain number of lords of appeal required at hearing and determination of appeals ; and (4) the appointment of Lords of Appeal in Ordinary by Her Majesty.

24 & 25 Vict. c. 133.
The second mode is shown in the principal and subordinate enactments found in the Land Drainage Act, 1861, in which the section enunciating the principle provides, by reference to the subsequent clauses, that it must be made *on the recommendation of the commissioners,* and *on such application and subject to such conditions* as are therein-after mentioned. Parliament, therefore, in passing the first section, pledged itself to require the recommendation of the Commissioners, and in a less degree pledged itself to the requirement of an application by the proprietors and to the other conditions of the Act. On the other hand, in the case of the Appellate Jurisdiction Act, Parliament, in passing the first section, did not pledge itself to require a particular form of appeal or to require the attendance of the Lords of Appeal in Ordinary.

The selection of the one or the other of the above methods of dealing with a principal enactment accompanied with a series of subordinate enactments, depends on Parliamentary considerations of the same character as those on which the arrangement of principles of law depends. Sometimes it is expedient to fetter the principal enactment with a direct reference to subordinate enactments, in order to show that Parliament is not asked to carry the law beyond a certain limit. On the other hand, in many cases it is desirable to take the opinion of Parliament on the principal proposition in its barest form, and stripped of every possible detail that can distract attention, or lead to votes being given on a side issue, instead of on the principle involved. Such questions must be determined by the Minister, rather than by a draftsman, but it is impossible to overrate their importance, as an Act not unfrequently is lost or won according as a division is taken on the right point and at the right time, on a simple or on a complicated issue.

9

Where political and Parliamentary considerations are not concerned, it is perhaps, on the whole, most convenient to introduce into the principal enactment references to the succeeding enactments, as the reader recollects a series of enactments when connected by referential words more readily than a chain of unconnected provisions.

Proceeding from the principle to the arrangement of the remainder of the Act the draftsman will find himself assisted by the following rules, first, in sifting his materials in such a manner as to enable him to form a clear conception of the subject matter with which he is dealing, and of the relations of its several parts to each other; and, secondly, in the practical task of arranging the sections of his Act and grouping them under appropriate headings. **8. GENERAL RULES OF ARRANGEMENT OF ACT, RULE I.**

Rule I.—Provisions declaring the law should be separated from and take precedence of provisions relating to the administration of the law.

Taking as an example the Bankruptcy Act, 1869, an analysis of which will be found in Appendix I., Part 1., it will be seen that Parts I. and II. of the Act, relating to the mode in which a man is made bankrupt, are separated from Part III., which contains the authority constituted to administer the law. Similarly in the Land Transfer Act, 1875, it will be found that the provisions relating to registration of title are contained in the first four parts of the Act, whilst the administration of the law stands by itself in the fifth part. **32 & 33 Vict. c. 71. 38 & 39 Vict. c. 87.**

The first part of the above rule is founded on the consideration that it is convenient for the purpose of clearness to separate the law from the authority to administer the law, and the reason for giving precedence to the law over administration is that until the law to be administered is determined the proper authority to administer that law cannot be judged of. Any verbal difficulty created by referring to the administrative authority before its constitution is stated may be avoided by the use on the occasion of the first mention of the authority of the phrases "the court by this Act constituted," " the commissioners in this Act referred to," or other referential phrases. The latter part of the rule, however, giving precedence to the law over the authority which administers the law is only applicable to a limited number of cases. Frequently the subject matter is of such a character as to require the authority to precede the law. Take, for example, the law as to coroner, the better mode would seem to be to create the coroner before laying down the law of inquest, on the ground that the law would seem to be an emanation from the authority, rather than the authority an institu-

I 92. B

tion established for administering an antecedent law. A similar observation would apply to an Act relating to sheriffs. In short, the rule is subject to so many exceptions that it is stated principally on the ground that any rule in so complicated a matter as legislation affords assistance to the draftsman, although it admits only of partial application.

28 & 29 Vict. c. 126. A notable example of a case in which the above-mentioned rule of putting the law before the administration has not been followed is found in the Prison Act, 1865. That Act begins by declaring the local bodies on whom is imposed by common law or by statute the obligation to maintain prisons. It then proceeds to lay down the rules with respect to the appointment of officers, the discipline of prisoners, and other matters relating to the prison, whilst it relegates to Part II. the law of prisons.

The reason for this disregard of the general rule was that in the particular case of prisons the law was altogether subordinate in importance to the provisions relating to the establishment of prisons, and it was thought advisable to submit to Parliament the important questions relating to the maintenance and administration of prisons, in preference to beginning with the comparatively insignificant and little known provisions relating to the law.

9. GENERAL RULES OF ARRANGEMENT OF ACT, RULE 2. *Rule II.—The simpler proposition should precede the more complex and in an ascending scale of propositions the lesser come before the greater.*

For example, in an Act relating to offences against property, theft should precede theft with violence, or robbery, and so forth; similarly, in dealing with the authority to administer the law, the lesser should precede the greater, the local the central, **38 & 39 Vict. c. 55.** *e.g.,* in the Public Health Act, 1875, the sanitary authority is dealt with before the Local Government Board.

This rule also is in a great measure arbitrary and suggested with a view of enabling the draftsman to form a clear conception of the relative bearing of sections, rather than to make it imperative on him to adopt it on all occasions. Such a rule must constantly yield to political pressure, and the draftsman is frequently required by his instructions, or by the special circumstances of the case, to put the more complex proposition before the less complex, or the higher authority before the lower.

On the whole, however, experience would seem to suggest that the observance of the rule leads to clearness and brevity in drawing; and uniformity in Acts of Parliament is of so much consequence that it is most desirable that some general rule of arrangement should wherever practicable be adopted.

Rule III.—Ordinary provisions should be separated from supple- **10. GENERAL**
mental. The latter should be placed towards the end of the Act, **RULES OF**
while the former should occupy their proper position in the narrative **OF ACT,**
of the occurrence to which they refer. **RULE 3.**

Ordinary provisions are such enactments as are in all cases
required to carry into effect the material objects of the Act.
Supplemental provisions are framed with a view to supply vacan-
cies in offices, defects in procedure, and so forth, or to declare in
detail the mode of working out the principles which have previously been laid down. Taking as an illustration the Public
Health Act, 1875, the sections in Part II. constituting sanitary **38 & 39 Vict.**
districts and sanitary authorities are ordinary provisions; the **c. 55.**
sections in Part VIII. altering the areas of districts and referring
to the formation of united districts are supplemental provisions.

A still better example is found in the Bankruptcy Act, 1869. **32 & 33 Vict.**
The proceedings in bankruptcy detailed in the first three parts of **c. 71.**
the Act are ordinary provisions, as they are the enactments which
lay down the precise manner in which the proceedings in bankruptcy
will be carried on if the creditors appoint a trustee and committee
of inspection, and if no vacancy occur either in the office of
trustee or committeeman, and generally if every step be taken in
due time and in a legal manner, while the provisions in the fourth
part of the Act are supplemental provisions, inasmuch as they
declare what is to be done in the event of the failure of any link
in the regular chain of legal action, or else supply working details
which by reason of their raising no question of principle were
omitted in the former part of the Act.

In short, the recommendation as to the separation of the ordinary provisions and the supplemental provisions amounts to this,
that on the first mention of a series of legislative acts, it should
be assumed that everything proceeds in its ordinary course, that no
one concerned will die or become bankrupt or omit to do his duty,
and that no abnormal circumstance will occur.

This mode of arrangement will doubtless be objected to by
persons who are desirous of acquiring a partial knowledge of an
Act without reading the whole, as being defective by reason of its
not grouping under one head all the provisions relating to the same
subject-matter.

It has, however, a twofold advantage—first, as respects Parliament, of submitting to the Legislature material provisions on
which they may decide without being embarrassed with subordinate consequential regulations; secondly, as respects readers of
the Act, by enabling them to obtain readily an intelligible view
of the material provisions of the law before entering upon details

involving no question of principle and interesting only to persons actually engaged in legal business.

11. GENERAL RULES OF ARRANGEMENT OF ACT, RULE 4.

Rule IV.—(a) Local or exceptional provisions, (b) temporary provisions, and (c) provisions relating to repeal of Acts should be separated from the other enactments, and placed by themselves under separate headings.

38 & 39 Vict. c. 87.

A good illustration of local or exceptional provisions is found in the Land Transfer Act, 1875. In that Act, the local registries for the counties of Middlesex and Yorkshire are dealt with at the end as separate subject-matters. By thus treating them as an exception to the remainder of the Act confusion is avoided, and the provisions are found without difficulty, being arranged under a separate heading.

32 & 33 Vict. c. 71.

Taking the Bankruptcy Act, 1869, as an example of temporary provisions, the new court is defined in the body of the Act in the same manner as if no other court were intended to be dealt with, while the temporary jurisdiction of the existing court and the status of the existing officers are found in a separate part of the Act. These provisions should never be mixed up with the permanent enactments, but should be set apart by themselves, as in a short time they die off and leave the measure complete without them.

Examples of Repeal clauses are found at the end of almost every Act which disturbs existing statute law.

12. GENERAL RULES OF ARRANGEMENT OF ACT, RULE 5.

Rule V.—Procedure and matters of detail should be set apart by themselves, and should not, except under very special circumstances, find any place in the body of the Act.

The above-mentioned matters should either be enacted in a schedule, or what is far better (where possible) be left to be prescribed by a court or department of the Government. For example, in the Companies Act, 1862, the model regulations for a company are prescribed in the schedule; the rules for winding up companies are directed to be framed by the court.

25 & 26 Vict. c. 89.

25 & 26 Vict. c. 63.

By the Merchant Shipping Act Amendment Act, 1862, section 25, the Queen can by Order in Council make regulations as to lights, fog signals, and sailing rules, while in other Merchant Shipping Acts, the Board of Trade take large powers of making orders for regulating the mercantile marine. By the Bankruptcy Act, 1869, all matters of detail are left to the jurisdiction of the Lord Chancellor with the advice of the Chief Judge in Bankruptcy; in the Trade Marks Registration Act, 1875, the principles only of the registration are laid down in the Act, whilst the general rules pointing out the mode of registry and the

32 & 33 Vict. c. 71.

38 & 39 Vict. c. 91.

classification of trade marks are directed to be made by the Lord Chancellor.

The adoption of the system of confining the attention of Parliament to material provisions only, and leaving details to be settled departmentally, is probably the only mode in which parliamentary government can, as respects its legislative functions, be satisfactorily carried on. The province of Parliament is to decide material questions affecting the public interest, and the more procedure and subordinate matters can be withdrawn from their cognizance, the greater will be the time afforded for the consideration of the more serious questions involved in legislation. Any attempt to evade the vigilance of Parliament by relegating to departments important matters can always be prevented by requiring the rules made to be laid before Parliament before they come into force.

Subject then to the subordination of logical to political require- **13. SUMMARY OF GENERAL RULES OF ARRANGEMENT AND OBSERVATIONS.** ments before observed on, and to the directions as to the selection and statement of the principle or principles of law, the general arrangement of an Act will be as follows :—

(1.) Law, ordinary provisions.
(2.) Administration of law, ordinary provisions.
(3.) Supplemental provisions, (*a*) law and (*b*) administration.
(4.) Local and exceptional provisions.
(5.) Temporary provisions.
(6.) Repeal clauses.
(7.) Rules of procedure and matters of detail in a schedule.

Abundant illustrations of the foregoing rules will be found in the arrangement of the sections of the Merchant Shipping Act, 1854 (17 & 18 Vict. c. 104.); of the Metropolitan Building Act, 1855 (18 & 19 Vict. c. 122.); of the Land Drainage Act, 1861 (24 & 25 Vict. c. 133.); of the Companies Act, 1862 (25 & 26 Vict. c. 89.); of the Prison Act, 1865 (28 & 29 Vict. c. 126.); of the Bankruptcy Act, 1869 (32 & 33 Vict. c. 71.); of the Irish Church Act, 1869 (32 & 33 Vict. c. 42.); of the Slaughter-houses (Metropolis) Act, 1874 (37 & 38 Vict. c. 67.); of the Explosives Act, 1875 (38 & 39 Vict. c. 17.); of the Artizans and Labourers Dwellings Improvement Act, 1875 (38 & 39 Vict. c. 36.); of the Local Loans Act, 1875 (38 & 39 Vict. c. 83.); and of the Land Transfer Act, 1875 (38 & 39 Vict. c. 87.).

In some of the above Acts the rules have been partially deviated from for reasons which it is impossible to detail without entering on lengthy explanations unsuited to this work. One maxim should however be steadily borne in mind by the draftsman, that whatever deviation may be allowed in the arrangement of principles and heads of law as between themselves, the essential conditions of a well drawn Act of Parliament are that every principle of law and every head of law should be separated from every other principle and head of law, and should form the subject of a separate enactment or series of enactments, and that in framing any enactment or series of enactments, the principle or head of law contained in such enactment or enactments should be stated at the outset, and the mode of giving effect to that principle or head of law should be dealt with by subordinate enactments, or otherwise according to circumstances.

Frequently, when the draftsman has sifted the materials of his Act according to the foregoing rules, and is about to turn his attention to the enactments, he will find a difficulty in ascertaining their mutual relations to each other ; in other words, the subject, although reduced in bulk, is still too large for him to classify throughout. His course here is to work out separately and in complete detail each head of the law as if it constituted the whole subject-matter of the Act. Such a course necessarily involves a great deal of labour, but when the process is completed he will see the mutual relations of the several parts of the Act, and will frequently be able to generalize his Act to a degree he could not have anticipated until he had completed the separate groups. *Divide et impera* is the motto of a draftsman as well as of a conqueror. The one thing needful is to make each distinct subject the matter of a separate section, or, if necessary, a separate series of sections, and not at the commencement to aim at conciseness when conciseness is placed in competition with or in antagonism to clearness of expression, or fulness in working out the details of the law.

Having completed his arrangement of an Act with the whole subject in his mind, the draftsman should scarcely ever alter it materially of his own accord. The consequence of such an alteration is to leave a confused outline of the law, which shows itself in the repetition or omission of necessary provisions, and in a hazy arrangement of the whole Act.

14. OBSERVATIONS ON REFERENTIAL PROVISIONS WHERE REFERENCE MADE TO ANOTHER PART OF THE SAME ACT. Before quitting the subject of arrangement it may be well to notice a constantly recurring difficulty in planning Acts and constructing sections, namely, the determination of the best mode of dealing with legal subjects which require similar but not identical provisions.

No general rule can be laid down for all cases, but the following suggestions may be useful. Where the provisions of the principal subject are applicable to the subordinate, with few and well defined exceptions, the best mode would seem to be to pursue the principal subject to its end without regard to the subordinate subject, and then to introduce a clause applying the provisions of the principal to the subordinate subject with certain exceptions.

For example, the provisions of the Bishops Resignation Act, 1869, were drawn as if they related only to English bishoprics, although it was intended from the first to extend them to the bishopric of Sodor and Man and to archbishoprics. This application to the two subordinate subjects of the provisions relating to the principal subject is made by s. 11 in the case of Sodor and Man as follows :—

32 & 33 Vict. c. 111.

> " This Act shall apply to the bishopric of Sodor
> " and Man in the same manner in all respects as if it
> " were a bishopric in England, with the following
> " exceptions:
>
> " (1.) If," &c.
> " (2.) If," &c.
> " (3.) The Bishop of Sodor and Man shall not," &c.

And in the case of the archbishoprics by s. 12 as follows :

> " A bishop coadjutor may be appointed in the case
> " of an archbishop being incapacitated by reason of
> " permanent mental infirmity from the due perform-
> " ance of his duties, in the same manner in all re-
> " spects as if such archbishop were a bishop and his
> " archbishopric a bishopric, and all the provisions of
> " this Act shall apply accordingly, with the following
> " additions and exceptions :
>
> " (1.) That," &c.
> " (2.) That," &c.
> " (3.) That," &c.

On a similar principle, the sixth and seventh parts of the Companies Act, 1862, apply the Act to companies existing at the passing of the Act.

25 & 26 Vict. c. 89.

Where English Acts are intended to be applied to Scotland and Ireland, confusion is avoided by omitting all special Scotch or Irish terms in the body of the Act, and adding at the end,—

" The provisions of this Act shall apply to Scotland (or Ireland, " as the case may require), with the following modifications ; that " is to say," and then setting out the modifications.

This is done very skilfully with respect to Scotland by the 58th section of the Parliamentary Elections Act, 1868, on the other hand the Irish special-law terms are inartistically mingled with the English throughout that Act.

31 & 32 Vict. c. 125.

The use of a generic term with a defining clause will not unfrequently prevent the necessity of overloading an Act with the enumeration of special provisions relating to particular local authorities. For an example of this " The Contagious Diseases

32 & 33 Vict. (Animals) Act, 1869," section 9, may be referred to, which is as
c. 70. follows :—

" For the purposes of this Act, the respective dis-
" tricts, authorities, rates, or funds, and officers de-
" scribed in the second schedule to this Act, shall be
" the district, the local authority, the local rate, and
" the clerk of the local authority."

Take the Act without this section, and endeavour to insert the various authorities in the text, and it will be at once found that almost every section requires a long list of names with special provisions interspersed.

Where a certain portion of the provisions of the principal subject are applicable to the subordinate subject without alteration, and some are totally inapplicable, while others require alteration, the principal subject may be continued to its close, with the exception of the provisions which are applicable, with slight alterations, to both subjects. The subordinate subject may then be introduced, and the former provisions, which are wholly applicable, to the principal subject, be incorporated by reference. Lastly will follow the provisions applicable with slight alteration to the principal and subordinate subjects.

25 & 26 Vict. The 4th part of the Companies Act, 1862, illustrates the fore-
c. 89. going observations. The winding-up by the court is the principal subject. This is worked out to its close, with the exception of the provisions incorrectly called " supplemental provisions," being in effect provisions applicable, with slight alterations, to the subordinate subject, as well as to the principal subject, which are postponed.

Then follows the main subordinate subject, " voluntary winding-up," incorporating the powers of the liquidators (sections 133–7), which are specially drawn with a view to incorporation.

Winding-up subject to supervision, comes next to voluntary winding up, and the differences, or rather the resemblances, between that process of winding-up and the preceding processes are stated in sections 148–152. Lastly come the " supplemental provisions," making general regulations applicable to all three systems.

32 & 33 Vict. Part VI. of the Bankruptcy Act, 1869, is another example of
c. 71. referential provisions. It adopts, so to speak, the whole of the previous provisions, with certain specified exceptions.

In whatever manner referential sections are arranged, great care and skill are required in making the referential words take up the principal enactments at the proper points, and the maxim that repetition is better than ambiguity should be constantly borne in mind.

In any event the draftsman should not be satisfied that he has

properly accomplished his task until he has read through the
principal enactments with the modifications proposed by the
referential expressions, and finds that when so read they effect
the object proposed.

However great his difficulty, the draftsman must exclude any
necessity for the adoption of the rule of "reddendo singula
singulis," or reading the sentences distributively; a rule which,
like other rules of construction, has arisen from the obligation
imposed on the courts of attaching an intelligible meaning to
confused and unintelligible sentences.

Referential provisions will naturally find a place at the close of
the enactments to which they are referential.

The referential legislation mentioned above, in which enactments
in one part of an Act refer to or incorporate wholly or partially
enactments contained in another part of the same Act must be
distinguished from referential legislation in which enactments in
one Act refer to or incorporate wholly or partially another Act
or Acts. The last-mentioned mode of legislation is proper or
improper according to circumstances. It is proper where the
object of the reference is to incorporate certain general Acts, or
parts of general Acts made for and adapted to incorporation.
For example, when powers of acquiring land are proposed to be
taken, the Lands Clauses Consolidation Act, 1845, must be incorporated with the proper modifications adapted to the cases of
voluntary or compulsory powers of purchase. Again, in all Acts
imposing small penalties the Summary Jurisdiction Acts must be
attracted. Loans by local authorities will be raised in manner
provided by the Local Loans Act, 1875.

Other instances may be cited, and it is the duty of a draftsman
to make himself thoroughly acquainted with all general Acts required to be incorporated, and with the best form of incorporating
them, and he ought not, without express instructions, to deviate
from or modify the provisions of the incorporated Acts, which
are well understood, and are capable of being incorporated without
creating any difficulty or raising any question of construction.

The advantages and disadvantages of incorporating a large
number of Consolidation Acts will be best learnt by comparing a
number of local Acts to which the series of Acts called the Consolidation Acts of 1845 and 1847 are applicable. The advantages
are that it secures uniformity of legislation and saves the time of
Parliament. The disadvantages are that it reduces an Act to a
mere outline, presenting to the reader no clear view of the law,
and obliging him to fill in the details either from recollection or
by a tedious examination of a number of distinct Acts. No
doubt the system as adopted in private legislation is inadmissible

15. OBSER-
VATIONS ON
REFERENTIAL
PROVISIONS
WHEN REFER-
ENCE MADE TO
OTHER ACTS.

8 & 9 Vict.
c. 18.

11 & 12 Vict.
c. 43.
38 & 39 Vict.
c. 83.

in public Acts in its full extent, but it must not on that account be wholly set aside; for when the reference is to a distinct operation which is only subsidiary to the main objects of the Act, *e.g.*, the purchase of lands in a sanitary Act, or the borrowing of money in a municipal Act, the possibility of referring to a distinct Act regulating such an operation conduces to clearness, and prevents the time of Parliament being wasted in considering unnecessary details. It is the application of the principle of incorporation to cases to which it is unsuited, not its adoption in a great number of cases where it is useful, which is to be condemned.

The referential legislation to be always avoided consists in referring in one Act to provisions of another Act, which do not readily lend themselves to incorporation, and require to be referentially modified before they can be made to harmonize with the incorporating Act.

An example of this description to be noticed for the purpose of being avoided may be found in the Nitro-glycerine Act, 1869, section 6, which applies to searching for nitro-glycerine all the Gunpowder Acts relating to searching for gunpowder.

32 & 33 Vict. c. 113.

16. OBSERVA-TIONS ON REFERENTIAL WORDS.

As to Referential Words.—The expressions "herein-before" and "herein-after," and references to particular sections by their numbers, should be carefully avoided wherever practicable, for the position of sections is so frequently changed in the passage of an Act through the House of Commons that the expressions become inaccurate. Moreover the word "herein-before" is frequently ambiguous, as sometimes it refers to the section alone in which it is found, and sometimes to the Act itself.

The above observation does not, of course, apply to referring in a subsequent Act to sections of an Act which has already become law, inasmuch as no alteration can take place in their arrangement.

17. OBSER-VATIONS ON DIVISION OF ACTS INTO PARTS AND HEADINGS.

A few remarks may be made, in conclusion, on the division of Acts into parts, and the grouping of clauses under separate headings.

The first step in this direction was taken in the Consolidation Acts of 1845, which were most ably drawn by Mr. Booth, late Secretary of the Board of Trade, whilst holding the office of Counsel to the Speaker.

In these Acts separate groups of sections are prefaced with a statement—

"With respect to (*the subject-matter of the group of sections*), "be it enacted as follows:—(The sections forming the group being inserted without the introductory words "And be it enacted that," which, at that time, it was the practice to insert at the beginning of every section in the Act.)

The above plan of grouping sections may still be adopted with advantage where it is intended to enable provisions to be incorporated with other Acts (as was the case in the Consolidation Acts), or where in the same Acts certain provisions are to be applied to a different subject matter.

The division into parts, and the grouping under headings or titles, was adopted in the Merchant Shipping Act of 1854 on the model, in some degree, of the Code of New York, and, if used judiciously, it facilitates considerably the understanding of an Act. It is, however, a mistake to imagine that a mere mechanical subdivision into parts insures clearness, and in many recent Acts subdivision has been carried to excess. *17 & 18 Vict. c. 104.*

As a general rule the division into parts should only be used where the subject matter of the Act involves different heads of law, each of which might without impropriety form the subject matter of a separate Act, or contains classes of enactments such as " Supplemental Provisions," or " Temporary Provisions " distinct in their character from the rest of the Act.

It may be well to mention here that where it is intended to refer in the enactments themselves to the division into parts, as, for example, by using the expressions " this part," " part five," or so forth, the Act itself should commence (as is the case in the Merchant Shipping Act, 1854, and in the Companies Act, 1862), by declaring that the Act is to be divided into parts, and specifying them. It will thus be out of the power of courts of law to refuse to recognise the division into parts, as being a substantive portion of the Act. *17 & 18 Vict. c. 104. 25 & 26 Vict. c. 89.*

The use of headings or titles dividing groups of sections also requires great care. If they are unnecessarily multiplied, they become little more than marginal notes; on the other hand, if clauses are grouped under them, which do not properly fall within the description of the heading, the reader is misled instead of being assisted.

Marginal notes should receive more attention than is usually given to them. Each note should express in a concise form the main object of the section on which it is made, or should at least indicate distinctly its subject matter; and all the notes, when read together in the " Arrangement of sections " should have such a consecutive meaning as will give a tolerably accurate idea of the contents of the Act. *18. OBSERVATIONS ON MARGINAL NOTES.*

CHAPTER III.

COMPOSITION OF SENTENCES.*

19. CLEARNESS. OBJECT OF PARLIAMENTARY DRAWING. Clearness is the main object to be aimed at in drawing Acts of Parliament. Clearness depends, first, on the proper selection of words; secondly, on the arrangement and the construction of sentences.

20. ENACTMENT IN ITS SIMPLEST FORM CONSISTS OF LEGAL SUBJECT AND LEGAL PREDICATE. An enactment in its simplest form is a declaration of the legislature, directing or empowering the doing or abstention from doing of a particular act or thing. Such an enactment consists of a legal subject and legal predicate. The legal subject denotes either the person directed or empowered to do or prohibited from doing the thing mentioned, or when the passive form is used the thing to be done or left undone. The legal predicate expresses what the person is to do or leave undone, or when the passive form is used what is enacted with respect to the thing to be done or to be left undone. If the law is imperative, the proper auxiliary verb of the predicate is "shall" or "shall not," if permissive, "may." For example :—

Subject.	Predicate.
Every Court	*shall* take judicial notice of the seal of the Bankruptcy Court.
This Act	*may be* cited as " The Companies Act, 1862."
A sheriff	*shall not*, after the commencement of this Act, be liable for the escape of a prisoner.

The expressions "It shall be lawful," "It is the duty," and similar impersonal forms, should not be used when the auxiliary verbs " shall," " shall not," or " may " will do equally well. Sometimes it is useful to substitute " It shall be lawful" for the auxiliary form of expression, in order that verbs in the infinitive mood may be used in the dependent sentences. The inclination of the Courts to construe " may " as sometimes imperative in an Act of Parliament requires that in doubtful cases the draftsman should add words such as " The Court may *in its discretion*," or " may *if it thinks it expedient*," and so forth. Where it is intended that a person should be exempted from the obligation to do a thing to which he would generally be subject (a very rare form of expression), it would be well to say " It shall be lawful for A.B. not to do so and so," as the phrase " may not " would

* *Note.*—See Coode's " Legislative Expression, or the Language of the written Law," a work which draftsmen are recommended to read, and to which I am much indebted in writing the instructions contained in this Chapter.

·imply a command that he should not do it. It is almost needless to add that expressions such as "may and are hereby required" are redundant, and should never be used.

A number of legal subjects, legal predicates, or independent enactments may be conveniently grouped together. Useful formulas for uniting such groups of legal subjects are as follows:—

    "After the commencement of this Act the follow-
    "ing persons; (that is to say,)

Legal subject, No. 1.   "(1.) Any person who has contracted to buy for
    "his own benefit an estate in fee simple in land,
    "whether subject or not to incumbrances; and

Legal subject, No. 2.   "(2.) Any person entitled for his own benefit at
    "law or in equity to an estate in fee simple in
    "land, whether subject or not to incumbrances;
    "and

Legal subject, No. 3.   "(3.) Any person capable of disposing for his own
    "benefit by way of sale of an estate in fee
    "simple in land, whether subject or not to in-
    "cumbrances,

Legal predicate.   "may apply to the registrar under this Act to be
    "registered.

"The following offenders; that is to say,
Legal subject.   "1. Any person who, &c.
Legal subject.   "2. Any person, who, &c.
Legal predicate.   "shall for each offence be liable to a fine not exceed-
    "ing

Legal subject.   "The Lord Chancellor, with the concurrence of
    "the Commissioners of Her Majesty's Treasury,
    "shall have power by general orders from time to
    "time to do all or any of the following things:
Legal predicate, No. 1.   "(1.) To create district registries, &c.;
Legal predicate, No. 2.   "(2.) To direct, by notice, &c.;
Legal predicate, No. 3.   "(3.) To commence registration, &c.;
Legal predicate, No. 4.   "(4.) To appoint district registrars, &c.
Legal subject.   The Lord Chancellor may, with the like concur-
Legal predicate.   rence, from time to time make, rescind, alter, or add to any order made in pursuance of this section."

Independent enactments of a simple character may be linked together by any of the following formulas:—

"The following consequences shall ensue upon the voluntary
  "winding up of a company.

21. Mode of grouping legal subjects. Land Transfer Act, 1875, 38 & 39 Vict. c. 87. s. 5.

The Merchant Shipping Act, 1854, 17 & 18 Vict. c. 104. ss. 322 and 323.

22. Mode of grouping legal predicates. Land Transfer Act, 1875, 38 & 39 Vict. c. 87. s. 118.

23. Mode of grouping independent enactments of a simple character. Companies Act, 1862, 25 & 26 Vict. c. 89. s. 133.

Companies
Act, 1862,
25 & 26 Vict.
c. 89. s. 174.
Land Transfer
Act, 1875,
38 & 39 Vict.
c. 87. s. 83.
Merchant Ship-
ping Act,
1854, 17 & 18
Vict. c. 104.
s. 103.

" The registration of companies under this Act shall be con-
" ducted as follows ; that is to say,

" The following enactments shall be made with respect to
" registration of title :—

" The offences herein-after mentioned shall be punishable as
" follows ; that is to say,"—

Sometimes a number of short enactments cannot conveniently
be arranged in subsections, and in such instances they may be
grouped in one section in the following manner :—

Artizans and
Labourers
Dwellings
Improvement
Act, 1875.
38 & 39 Vict.
c. 36. s. 5.

Enactment, No. 1.

" The improvement scheme of a local authority
" shall be accompanied by maps, particulars, and esti-
" mates ;

Enactments, No. 2 & 3.

" it may exclude any part of the area in respect of
" which an official representation is made, or include
" any neighbouring lands, if the local authority are of
" opinion that such exclusion is expedient or inclu-
" sion is necessary for making their scheme efficient
" for sanitary purposes ;

Enactment, No. 4.

" it may also provide for widening any existing ap-
" proaches to the unhealthy area or otherwise for open-
" ing out the same for the purposes of ventilation or
" health ;

Enactment, No. 5.

" also it shall distinguish the lands proposed to be
" taken compulsorily, and shall provide for the accom-
" modation of at the least as many persons of the
" working class as may be displaced in the area with
" respect to which the scheme is proposed, in suit-
" able dwellings, which, unless there are any special
" reasons to the contrary, shall be situate within the
" limits of the same area, or in the vicinity thereof ;

Enactment, No. 6.

" it shall also provide for proper sanitary arrange-
" ments ;

Enactment, No. 7.

" it may also provide for such scheme or any part
" thereof being carried out and effected by the person
" entitled to the first estate of freehold in any pro-
" perty subject to the scheme or with the concurrence
" of such person, under the superintendence and con-
" trol of the local authority, and upon such terms and
" conditions to be embodied in the scheme as may
" be agreed upon between the local authority and
" such person."

An instance of the advantage of grouping enactments in a 32 & 33 Vict. matter of some complexity may be found in the Irish Church Act, c. 42. s. 40. 1869.

" When the annual sums herein-after mentioned
" cease to be paid, compensation shall be made in
" respect thereof by payment of capital sums as
" follows ; that is to say,

" (1.) In respect of the annual sum paid out, &c.,
" by payment of the capital sum herein-after
" mentioned to, &c. :

" (2.) In respect of the several annual sums paid
" out of, &c. (such sums to be ascertained on
" an average of such number of years as the
" Commissioners may think fit) by payment
" of the capital sums herein-after mentioned
" to, &c. :

" (3.) In respect of the several sums paid annually
" by, &c., by payment of the capital sum
" herein-after mentioned to, &c. :

" (4.) In respect of the annual sum paid out of, &c.
" by payment of the capital sum herein-after
" mentioned to, &c. :

" (5.) In respect of the annual sums granted, &c.,
" by payment of the capital sum herein-after
" mentioned to, &c. :

" (6.) In respect of the buildings of the said college,
" by payment of a sum   :

" (7.) In respect of the annual sums granted, &c.,
" by payment of the capital sum herein-after
" mentioned to, &c.:

" (8.) In respect of the annual sum paid, &c., by
" payment of the capital sum herein-after
" mentioned to, &c."

Little difficulty would arise in framing Acts of Parliament if **24. MODE OF** the law were, as a general rule, meant to apply universally. It is, **STATING THE** however, usually limited to special cases, and the first duty of a **CASE.** draftsman is to state clearly the nature of the case to which the law applies.

Where the case is simple it should be introduced at the beginning of the section with the words " where " or " when," " in the event of " or " if," with the indicative.

Case.   " Where any company is being wound up,   The Companies
Statutory   " all books, accounts, and documents of the company   Act, 1862.
declaration.   " and of the liquidators shall, as between the contri-   25 & 26 Vict. c. 89. ss. 111, 154.

24

" butories of the company, be primâ facie evidence
" of the truth of all matters purporting to be therein
" recorded.

Case.　" When the affairs of the company have been com-
" pletely wound up.

Statutory　" the court shall make an order that the company be
declaration(1).　" dissolved from the date of such order,

Statutory　" and the company shall be dissolved accordingly."
declaration(2).

Where a single statutory declaration applies to numerous cases,
it is convenient to arrange them as follows:—

25 & 26 Vict.　Statutory　" A company under this Act may be wound up
c 89. s. 79.　declaration.　" by the court, as herein-after defined, under the fol-
" lowing circumstances ; (that is to say,)

Cases.　" (1.) Whenever, &c.
" (2.) Whenever, &c.
" (3.) Whenever, &c.
" (4.) Whenever, &c.
" (5.) Whenever," &c.

25 & 26 Vict.　Statutory　" The expression 'the court,' as used in this part
c. 89. s. 81.　declaration.　" of this Act, shall mean the following authorities;
" (that is to say,)

Cases.　" In the case of a company, &c.
" In the case of a company, &c.
" In the case of a company, &c.
" In all cases of companies, &c.
" Provided that, &c."

Sometimes a statement of the cases precedes the statutory
declaration :—

Cases.　" In the following cases ; that is to say,
Statutory
declaration.　" (1.) Where, &c.
" (2.) Where, &c.
" (3.) Where, &c."

A useful example of a case with subordinate clauses stating
alternatives and several statutory declarations is found in the
Foreign Enlistment Act, 1870 (33 & 34 Vict., c. 90. s. 7.), as
follows:—

Case with sub-　" If the master or owner of any ship, without
ordinate
clauses.　" the license of Her Majesty, knowingly either takes
" on board, or engages to take on board, or has on
" board such ship within Her Majesty's dominions,
" any of the following persons, in this Act referred
" to as illegally enlisted persons; that is to say,
" (1.) Any person who, &c.

"(2.) Any person, being a British subject, who, &c.

"(3.) Any person who, &c.

Statutory declaration No. 1.

"Such master or owner shall be guilty of an "offence against this Act, and the following conse-"quences shall ensue; that is to say,

Statutory declaration No. 2.

"(1.) The offender shall be punishable by fine and "imprisonment, or either of such punishments, "at the discretion of the court before which the "offender is convicted; and imprisonment, if "awarded, may be either with or without hard "labour; and

Statutory declaration No. 3.

"(2.) Such ship shall be detained until the trial "and conviction or acquittal of the master or "owner, and until all penalties inflicted on the "master or owner have been paid, or the "master or owner has given security for the "payment of such penalties to the satisfaction "of two justices of the peace, or other magis-"trate or magistrates having the authority of "two justices of the peace; and

Statutory declaration No. 4.

"(3.) All illegally enlisted persons shall imme-"diately on the discovery of the offence be "taken on shore, and shall not be allowed to "return to the ship."

A case with several alternatives may be expressed as follows:—Merchant Shipping Act, 1854, 17 & 18 Vict. c. 104. s. 45.

Case.

"Whenever any change takes place in the regis-"tered ownership of any ship, then, if such change "occurs at a time when the ship is at her port of "registry,

Statutory declaration.

"the master shall forthwith deliver the certificate of "registry to the registrar, and he shall endorse thereon "a memorandum of such change;

Alternative Case.

"but if such change occurs during the absence of the "ship from her port of registry,

Statutory declaration.

"then upon her first return to such port the master "shall deliver the certificate of registry to the regis-"trar, and he shall endorse thereon a like memorandum "of the change;

Further alternative case.

"or if she previously arrives at any port where there "is a *British* registrar,

Statutory declaration (1).

"such registrar shall, upon being advised by the "registrar of her port of registry of the change

I 92.

C

"having taken place, endorse a like memorandum
"thereof on the certificate of registry, and may for
"that purpose require the certificate to be delivered to
"him, so that the ship be not thereby detained;

Statutory declaration (2). "and any master who fails to deliver to the registrar the
"certificate of registry as herein-before required shall
"incur a penalty not exceeding one hundred pounds."

General rule as to expression of case. The case must always be so expressed as to be clearly distinguishable from the other parts of the sentence; but it need not, indeed should not, where the rules of composition require a different arrangement, be comprised in a consecutive sentence. A separation of the members of a case is almost always desirable where it consists partly of the statement of a fact and partly of an act to be done. This will appear from the following example, in which the case is shown in italics, the statutory declaration in ordinary type.

Irish Church Act, 1869. 32 & 33 Vict. c. 42. s. 25, sub-section 3. "*Where any church was in use at the time of the passing of this
"Act, and no application in respect thereof is made by the said
"representative body of the said church within the said prescribed
"period, and such church was erected at the private expense of any
"person,* the Commissioners shall, *on the application of the person
"who erected such church, if alive, or of his representatives if he
"died since the year one thousand eight hundred,* by order vest
"such church in the applicant or applicants, or in such person or
"persons as he or they may direct."

25. MODE OF STATING CONDITIONS. The law frequently confers a benefit or imposes an obligation on certain conditions; a condition is aptly introduced by "If, &c.," or (where it follows a negative sentence) by "unless" or "until."

Case. "Where any person is convicted of an offence
Condition. "if he has given notice at the prescribed time and
"in the prescribed manner
Statutory declaration. "he may appeal from such conviction, &c."

32 & 33 Vict. c. 42. s. 34. Where the conditions are numerous it is best (as has been before remarked with respect to the case) to state them in separate subordinate sentences.

Statutory declaration. "The Commissioners may at any time after the
"first of January one thousand eight hundred and
"seventy-one sell by public auction or private con-
"tract, or otherwise convert into money, any real or
"personal property vested in them by this Act,
Conditions. "subject to the other provisions of this Act, and
"to the following conditions:
"(1.) They shall not sell, &c.

" (2.) Perpetuity rents shall, &c.
" (3.) The price of the rights to mines or quarries
" shall, &c.
" (4.) They shall not sell to the public, &c.
" (5.) They shall not sell to the public, &c.
" (6.) Notice shall be given to, &c.
" (7.) An owner shall be deemed, &c."

Case.

" Where any person is authorised by any Act of
" Parliament passed after the commencement of this
" Act to appeal from the decision of a court of summary
" jurisdiction to a court of general or quarter sessions,

Statutory declaration.

" he may appeal to such court,

" subject to the conditions and regulations following

Condition 1.   " (1.) The appeal shall be made, &c.
Condition 2.   " (2.) The appellant shall, &c.
Condition 3.   " (3.) The appellant shall, &c.
Condition 4.   " (4.) Where the appellant, &c.
Condition 5.   " (5.) The court of appeal, &c.
Condition 6.   " (6.) Whenever a decision, &c.
Condition 7.   " (7.) Every notice, &c."

Another mode of stating the conditions in the last-mentioned example would be to substitute for the words " subject to the " conditions and regulations following " the words " but no appeal " shall be entertained *unless* the following conditions and regula- " tions have been complied with." The greatest caution must, however, be used in putting a sentence in a negative form, as it makes the performance of the conditions a matter of absolute necessity, and the omission of the smallest portion of them will render the appeal altogether nugatory. On the other hand, if the affirmative expression only be used the court will consider the enactment as to the conditions directory, and dispense with them on due cause being shown for their omission.

In the Bankruptcy Act, 1869, section 48, it is intended that 32 & 83 Vict. the court should have no power to discharge a bankrupt unless some c. 71. s. 48. one of the conditions therein mentioned have been complied with.

Accordingly the forty-eighth section is worded as follows :—

Cases. 1 2

" When a bankruptcy is closed, or at any time " during its continuance, with the assent of the " creditors testified by a special resolution

Statutory declaration.

" the bankrupt may apply to the court for an order " of discharge but such discharge shall not be granted

Alternative conditions.

" *unless it is proved to the court that one of the fol-* " *lowing conditions has been fulfilled, that is to say,*

c 2

" *either that a dividend of not less than ten shillings*
" *in the pound has been paid out of his property, or*
" *might have been paid except through the negligence or*
" *fraud of the trustee, or that a special resolution of*
" *his creditors has been passed to the effect that his*
" *bankruptcy or the failure to pay ten shillings in the*
" *pound has, in their opinion, arisen from circumstances*
" *for which the bankrupt cannot justly be held respon-*
" *sible, and that they desire that an order of discharge*
" *should be granted to him.*"

38 & 39 Vict. c. 36. An example of very complicated cases, with a condition, attached to the later but not to the earlier statutory declaration, may be found in the Artizans and Labourers Dwellings Improvement Act, 1875, section 3.

26. MODE OF STATING EXCEPTIONS. The word "except" may generally be used in introducing exceptions, but care must be taken to avoid its use where it is likely to lead to ambiguity. This is illustrated by the fourteenth section of the Irish Church Bill as brought in. That section was as follows :—

" The Commissioners shall, as soon as may be after
" the passing of this Act, ascertain and declare by
" order the amount of yearly income of which the
" holder of any archbishopric, bishopric, benefice, or
" cathedral preferment in or connected with the said
" Church will be deprived by virtue of this Act,
" after deducting all rates and taxes, *except income*
" *or property tax, salaries of permanent curates em-*
" *ployed as herein-after mentioned, payments to dio-*
" *cesan schoolmasters, and other outgoings to which*
" *such holder is liable by law.*"

In the above example it will be perceived that it was intended only to except income or property tax, but as the sentence is worded it may reasonably be argued that all the substantives that follow the word "except" are excepted. The sentence should run as follows :

" After deducting all rates and taxes, salaries to
" permanent curates employed as herein-after men-
" tioned, payments to diocesan schoolmasters, and
" other outgoings to which such holder is liable by
" law, but not deducting income or property tax."

Where exceptions are numerous they should (as in the instances of numerous cases and numerous conditions) be placed in separate members of the section or even in a separate section. Where the enumeration of the exceptions is short, compared with the enumeration of the particulars not excepted, it is often convenient to state the exceptions first. Illustrations of this may be found in the fifteenth and thirty-first sections of the Bankruptcy Act, 1869.

32 & 33 Vict. c. 71.

" The property of the bankrupt divisible amongst s. 15.
" his creditors, and in this Act referred to as the
" property of the bankrupt, shall not comprise the
" following particulars :

Exception 1.   " (1.) Property held by the bankrupt on trust for
" any other person :

Exception 2.   " (2.) The tools (if any) of his trade, and the
" necessary wearing apparel and bedding of
" himself, his wife and children, to a value,
" inclusive of tools and apparel and bedding,
" not exceeding twenty pounds in the
" whole :"

But it shall comprise the following particulars :

General enumeration.   " (3.) All such property as may belong to or be
" vested in the bankrupt at the commence-
" ment of the bankruptcy, or may be ac-
" quired by or devolve on him during its
" continuance :
" (4.) The capacity to exercise and take proceedings
" for exercising all such powers in or over
" or in respect of property as might have
" been exercised by the bankrupt for his
" own benefit at the commencement of his
" bankruptcy or during its continuance, ex-
" cept the right of nomination to a vacant
" ecclesiastical benefice :
" (5.) All goods and chattels being, at the com-
" mencement of the bankruptcy, in the pos-
" session, order, or disposition of the bank-
" rupt, being a trader, by the consent and
" permission of the true owner, of which
" goods and chattels the bankrupt is reputed
" owner, or of which he has taken upon
" himself the sale or disposition as owner ;
" provided that things in action, other than
" debts due to him in the course of his
" trade or business, shall not be deemed
" goods and chattels within the meaning of
" this clause."

<table>
<tr><td>32 & 33 Vict.
c. 71, s. 31.</td><td>Further
Exceptions.</td><td>" Demands in the nature of unliquidated damages
" arising otherwise than by reason of a contract or
" promise shall not be provable in bankruptcy, and no
" person having notice of any act of bankruptcy
" available for adjudication against the bankrupt shall
" prove for any debt or liability contracted by the
" bankrupt subsequently to the date of his so having
" notice.</td></tr>
</table>

Further
enumeration.

" Save as aforesaid, all debts and liabilities, present
" or future, certain or contingent, to which the bank-
" rupt is subject at the date of the order of adjudi-
" cation, or to which he may become subject during
" the continuance of the bankruptcy by reason or
" any obligation incurred previously to the date of
" the order of adjudication, shall be deemed to be
" debts provable in bankruptcy, and may be proved
" in the prescribed manner before the trustee in the
" bankruptcy."

32 & 33 Vict.
c. 62, s. 4.

On the other hand, in the Debtors Act, 1869, section four,
the exceptions being numerous are placed at the end of the
section :—

Statutory
declaration.

" No person shall, after the commencement of this
" Act, be arrested or imprisoned for making default
" in payment of a sum of money.

" There shall be excepted from the operation of the
" above enactment :

Exception 1.   " 1. Default, &c.
Exception 2.   " 2. Default, &c.
Exception 3.   " 3. Default, &c.
Exception 4.   " 4. Default, &c.
Exception 5.   " 5. Default, &c.
Exception 6.   " 6. Default, &c."

27. USE OF PROVISOES.

Provisoes should never be used to define the case or the condition or the legal subject ; their proper function is to make a
special exemption from a general statutory declaration, and they
should be exclusively confined to that function. The rules with
respect to the grouping of conditions and exceptions apply to
provisoes also where they are numerous.

28. SUMMARY OF RULES.

To give a short summary of what has been stated. The
draftsman should recollect that an enactment, in its most complicated form, is made up of the following parts :—

(1.) The case ;
(2.) The statutory declaration ;

(3.) The conditions;

(4.) The exception;

(5.) The provisoes.

The arrangement of these parts must much depend on the judgment of the draftsman; the only general rule to be observed is that each part should in substance be clearly distinguishable, and should be comprised, as far as possible, in a short sentence or sentences.*

It may be well to give a few miscellaneous suggestions with respect to the selection of words and structure of sentences.

29. Selection of words and other matters.

In the selection of words, Latin words and, where possible without a sacrifice of accuracy, technical phraseology should be avoided; the word best adapted to express a thought in ordinary composition will generally be found to be the best that can be used in an Act of Parliament.

The use of technical phraseology may be admitted in an Act relating to contingent remainders, but should in the case of an Agricultural Holdings Act or Highway Act be excluded from the body of the Act, and if required to be introduced for the purpose of securing legal precision, appear only in the interpretation clause explaining, extending, or limiting words in ordinary use, such as " Agricultural Holding," " Highway," and so forth. Law is made for man, and not man for law; and it is too often forgotten by lawyers and draftsmen that the greater number of Acts of Parliament contain rules of conduct to be observed by illiterate persons, and to be enforced by authorities unacquainted with the technical language of Coke and the year books.

A draftsman should pay attention to collecting and arranging for his own use any relative terms, such as " mortgage, mortgagor, " mortgagee," " comply, compliance," " require, requisition;" and exhaustive forms of expression, such as " all property, real " and personal, including all interests and rights in to or out of " property," " rights, duties, liabilities, capacities and incapacities " " acts, neglects, defaults."

The miscellaneous remarks following may be useful:

Nouns should be used in preference to pronouns, even though the noun has to be repeated. Repetition of the same word is never a fault in parliamentary drawing, if an ambiguity is thereby avoided.

---

* Where the circumstances under which an enactment is to take effect are complicated there is no practical difference, except in form, between the statement of the subordinate propositions of the case and conditions, and the draftsman must use his discretion in using one or the other form as he deems most advisable.

An Act of Parliament should be deemed to be **always** speaking and therefore the present or past tense should be adopted, and "shall" should be used as an *imperative* only, and not as a *future*. "If" should be followed by the indicative where it suggests a case; for example, "If any person commits, &c., he shall be "punished as follows."

Where there is an enumeration of several persons or things, followed by an enactment intended to apply to all and each of them, care must be taken to make this enactment apply both generally and distributively. For instance, "A., B., C., and D., "or any of them, may, &c.," or "any one or more of the following "persons may."

It must be recollected that "other" following an enumeration of various particulars is always construed to mean other things of the like description as those before enumerated, unless the construction be negatived by the introduction of words such as "whether of the same kind as, &c., or not."

Numbers should be written at full length; thus sections of an Act should be cited as "section two," &c. The titles, as well as the year and chapter of Acts should, for the sake of accuracy, be given, and where an Act is cited by its short title a reference should always be made in the margin to its session and chapter.

Lastly, the same thing should invariably be said in the same words.

30. RECOMMENDATION OF USE OF GENERIC TERMS.
32 & 33 Vict. c. 71. s. 31.

It will often be found that it is absolutely essential to shorten a sentence by giving a generic name to several particulars. Take for example section 31 of the Bankruptcy Act. The courts are extremely reluctant to give effect to general expressions; it was doubted therefore whether "debts and liabilities," explained as they are in the second sentence of that section, would be sufficient. Accordingly a separate definition of "liability" is given at the end of the section, in the following terms:—

"'Liability' shall for the purposes of this Act "include any compensation for work or labour done, "any obligation or possibility of an obligation to pay "money or money's worth on the breach of any express "or implied covenant, contract, agreement, or under- "taking, whether such breach does or does not occur, "or is or is not likely to occur or capable of occurring "before the close of the bankruptcy, and generally "it shall include any express or implied engagement, "agreement, or undertaking to pay, or capable of "resulting in the payment of money or money's "worth, whether such payment be, as respects

" amount, fixed or unliquidated; as respects time,
" present or future, certain, or dependent on any one
" contingency or on two or more contingencies ; as
" to mode of valuation, capable of being ascertained
" by fixed rules, or assessable only by a jury, or as
" matter of opinion."

Similarly, at section 91 of the same Act, " settlement'' is de- 32 & 33 Vict.
fined for the purpose of preventing a repetition of the numerous c. 71. s. 91.
words at the beginning of the sentence.

Not unfrequently a difficulty may be avoided by nicknaming,
as it were, a particular person or body of persons, so as to
comprise in one word what would otherwise make a complicated
sentence. Take for example the sixty-sixth section of the Prison
Act, 1865. That section is as follows :—

" Where a prison authority, in this section called 28 & 29 Vict.
" the contracting authority, has contracted with any c. 126. s. 66.
" other prison authority, in this section called the
" receiving authority, that the receiving authority is
" to receive into and maintain in its prison any
" prisoners maintainable at the expense of the con-
" tracting authority, the prison of the receiving autho-
" rity shall for all the purposes of and incidental to
" the commitment, trial, detention, and punishment of
" the prisoners of the contracting authority, or any of
" such purposes, according to the tenor of the contract,
" be deemed to be the prison of the contracting au-
" thority, except that the contracting authority shall
" have no right to interfere in the management of
" the prison of the receiving authority."

A little consideration will show that if the words " contracting 32 & 33 Vict.
authority," " receiving authority," were not adopted, the sentence c. 81.
would be overloaded with words to such an extent as to be unintelligible. In short, whenever a draftsman finds his sentence
becoming confused, although he has duly observed the directions
as to the statement of the case, the conditions, and so forth, he
may be certain that some part of it wants to be separated from
the rest, and to be dealt with as a separate paragraph at the
end of the section, or even as a separate section. The framer of 38 & 39 Vict.
the Volunteer Act, 1869, obviously saw the difficulty of stating c. 36.
in section three the mode in which the demand was to be made ;
as it comprised so many particulars, that it would, if introduced
into the beginning of that section, have inconveniently separated

the several members of the case. Accordingly he lightened section three by inserting in that section the words " on demand " made as herein-after mentioned," and placed the particulars of the demand in section four.

A similar course was adopted in " The Artizans and Labourers Dwellings Improvement Act, 1875." On referring to the Act it will be found that the action of the local authority under section three is to take place " when an official representation as hereinafter mentioned " is made as to the unhealthiness of the area, and so forth.

The nature of the official representation referred to in section three is stated in section four.

A reference to the Act will show that if section four had formed part of section three the case would have been so overcrowded with words as to be absolutely unintelligible.

17 & 18 Vict. c. 104. s. 346. A form of section that deserves to be considered by a draftsman, as an example of the advantage to be derived from getting a generic term to express and include a number of special predicates, is the following section of the Merchant Shipping Act, 1854.

" Every pilot boat or ship shall be distinguished by
" the following *characteristics ;* (that is to say,)
" (1.) A black colour painted or tarred outside, &c. :
" (2.) On her stern the name of the owner
" thereof and the port to which she belongs
" painted in white letters, and on each bow
" the number of the license of such boat
" or ship :
" (3.) When afloat, a flag at the mast-head or on
" a sprit, or staff, &c."
" And it shall be the duty of the master of such boat
" or ship to attend to the following *particulars :* First,
" that the boat or ship possesses all the above *charac-*
" *teristics ;* secondly, that the aforesaid flag is kept
" clean and distinct, so as to be easily discerned at a
" proper distance; and lastly, that the names and
" numbers before mentioned are not at any time
" concealed ; and if default is made in any of the
" above particulars he shall incur a penalty not ex-
" ceeding twenty pounds for each default."

The generic term *characteristics* prevents the necessity for a repetition of the sub-sections 1, 2, and 3. Similarly the declaration that " it shall be the duty of the master to attend to the

" following particulars," and the infliction of the penalty on default being made "in any of the above particulars," makes the master liable, first, for a general default in the boat not possessing the characteristics required ; and, secondly, for a special default in not attending to the flag being kept clean, and so forth.

Section 48 of the same Act illustrates the advantage of the use of the word " event " where a set of circumstances have to be repeated :—

> " *In the event* of the certificate of registry of any 17 & 18 Vict.
> " ship being mislaid, lost, or destroyed, if such *event* c. 104. s. 48.
> " occurs at any port in the United Kingdom, &c.,
> " then the registrar of her port of registry shall grant
> " a new certificate of registry in lieu of and as a
> " substitute for her original certificate of registry ;
> " but if such *event* occurs elsewhere, the master or
> " some other person having knowledge of the cir-
> " cumstances shall make a declaration, &c.; and
> " the registrar shall thereupon grant a provisional
> " certificate, &c."

If the word " event " were not used it would require a constant repetition of the words " certificate of registry of any ship being " mislaid, lost, or destroyed."

As to Enumeration of Particulars. — In framing an Act **31. Enumera-** intended to include a great number of particulars, no attempt **tion of Par-** should be made to enumerate the particulars, but a generic term **ticulars.** should be used dealing exhaustively with the subject-matter of the Act. Those particulars only should be enumerated which are intended to be excepted from the Act ; for example, the Succession Duty Act is framed with a view of including every disposition or devolution of property at death that is not subject to the Legacy Duty Acts. It was impossible to make any exhaustive enumeration of the particulars of the property to be included in the Act. The course, therefore, was adopted of including in the Act every possible disposition or devolution of property on death, and then to exempt from the operation of the Act any acquisition of property in respect of which duty was payable under the Legacy Duty Acts.

These illustrations might be multiplied indefinitely. The draftsman should read carefully Mr. Coode's book on legislative expression, before referred to, and should study, for forms of expression, the Code of Criminal Procedure and Civil Procedure of the State of New York, and the General Rules of the Court of Chancery of the 8th May 1845. He should also analyse the arrangement of Acts, and pick to pieces sentences which appear to him to be well drawn. As a model of clearness of expression no better example can be found than Paley's work on Moral Philosophy.*

CHAPTER IV.

GENERAL OBSERVATIONS.

The object of this chapter is to explain certain formal parts and groups of sections constantly recurring in Acts of Parliament.

32. PRE-AMBLE.

As to Preambles.—The proper function of a preamble is to explain certain facts which are necessary to be explained before the enactments contained in the Act can be understood; for

28 & 39 Vict. c. 48.

example, the Courts of Justice Building Act, 1865, proposes to apply certain funds to the payment of the expenses of constructing new courts of justice. Accordingly a long preamble is prefixed to the Act, explaining the origin of those funds; for without such a preamble it would have been impossible for Parliament to have understood the subject-matter of the Act. Preambles are also not unfrequently required in amending Acts for the purpose of showing the exact bearing of the amendments on the principal Act.

A preamble may also be used to limit the scope of certain expressions in an Act; for example, in dealing with the subject of licensing public houses, it may be convenient in the preamble to define as licensing Acts the Acts relating to the sale of intoxicating liquors.

Sometimes a preamble is inserted for political reasons when the object of an Act is popular, and admits of being stated in a telling sentence or sentences.

Other cases will occur in practice, in which a preamble will be found convenient to explain a fact or introduce a definition;

* The most frequent cause of ambiguity in Acts of Parliament is the want of an adjectival inflexion. For example, the expression " Every factory and every work-" shop subject to this Act," raises the question whether " subject to this Act " applies to both or to the last only of the nouns. If it is intended to apply to the last only, the ambiguity is avoided by placing the qualified noun before the unqualified, that is to say, by reading the sentence " Every workshop subject to this " Act and every factory." To make the qualification certainly apply to both the form of sentence must be altered somewhat in this way, " Where a factory and a " workshop are subject to this Act they shall," &c.

The same difficulty arises in the case of the relative, *e.g.*, " In a factory or work-" shop in which young children are employed," is an expression subject to the same ambiguity, which can only be avoided by adopting a similar rule to that recommended above, or else by repeating the antecedent, and reading the sentence, " Every factory " and workshop in which factory and workshop young children are employed.",

but it is not as a general rule adviseable to enunciate the principle
of an Act in a preamble, as the opponents of the Act are sure
to select it as a battle ground instead of dividing on the actual
provisions of the Act.

As to short title of Act.—Every Act should have a short title, **33. Short**
ending with the date of the year in which it is passed. **title of Act.**

In the absence of a short title it is necessary to quote the Act
as " an Act of the session of the   and   years of
" Her Majesty, chapter so-and-so, intituled so-and-so," and the
repetition of so long a title is extremely inconvenient if it frequently occurs. True it is that Lord Brougham's Act enables **13 & 14 Vict.**
reference to be made to a particular statute without mentioning **c. 21.**
its title, but it is very inexpedient to do so, as the mere insertion
of a particular chapter fails to convey to the mind of the reader
any idea of the Act referred to, and mistakes often arise from
a misprint in the number of a chapter.

As to extent of Act.—Where an Act is intended to operate **34. Extent**
within the territorial limits of the United Kingdom but not be- **of Act.**
yond, there is no necessity for a section declaring the extent of the
Act. The most frequent use of such a section is to restrict the Act
to England by declaring that it shall not extend to Scotland or
Ireland. Sometimes, however, an affirmative extension is required,
declaring that it is to extend to the Channel Islands, the Colonies,
Her Majesty's dominions in India, and so forth.

Wales and Berwick-upon-Tweed are included in England by
the Act of 20 Geo. 2. c. 42., and ought not therefore to be specially
mentioned. The phrase that an Act shall apply to " England
only " is not advisable, as it would seem to exclude by inference
the inclusion in England of Wales and Berwick-upon-Tweed
established by the above mentioned Act of 20 Geo. 2.

As to commencement of Act.—At common law every Act of **35. Com-**
Parliament commences from the first day of the session in which **mencement**
it is passed. The injustice arising from such a rule was obviated **of Act.**
by 33 Geo. 3. c. 13. which enacts that the Clerk of the Parlia-
ments shall endorse after the title of the Act the date, month, and
year when the same is passed and receives the Royal Assent, and
that such endorsement shall be taken to be part of such Act, and
to be the date of its commencement where no other commencement is therein provided. Even thus, great inconvenience arises
from bringing a complicated Act into operation immediately on
the date of its passing, and it is almost always advisable to
postpone its operation for some little time, in order at all events
that the public may become acquainted with its provisions. The
1st of January ensuing the passing of the Act is the most natural
day for bringing it into operation, when there are no special
reasons to be adduced in favour of another day. If, however,

38

the Act commences at a future perio·l there should usually be inserted a provision giving immediate effect to any rules, appointments of officers, or other machinery required to bring the Act duly into operation at the date of its commencement.

36. Construction of terms.

13 & 14 Vict. c. 21.

As to Construction of Act.—The interpretation clause should be preceded by a qualifying introductory clause, such as " In this " Act, unless the context otherwise requires." In framing definitions, regard must be had to the provisions of Lord Brougham's Act. Definitions require to be carefully considered, as a misuse of them is a frequent cause of ambiguity. It should be recollected that a word once defined preserves its meaning throughout the whole Act—a truism frequently overlooked in practice. A word should never be defined to mean something which it does not properly include, *e.g.*, " piracy " ought not to be defined to include " mutiny," and so forth. The fewer the definitions the better, and as a general rule, the draughtsman should endeavour to draw his Act without definitions, and insert them only when he finds that they are absolutely necessary. The proper use of definitions is to include or exclude something with respect to the inclusion or exclusion of which there is a doubt without such a definition, and no attempt should be made to make a pretence of scientific precision by defining words of which the ordinary meaning is sufficiently clear and exact for the purpose of the Act in which they are used.

37. As to place in Act of definitions and certain other preliminary matters.

32 & 33 Vict. c. 70. sch. 2.

As to all above-mentioned Sections. — The above-mentioned sections must be placed either at the beginning or the end of the Act. Logically, their proper place is the beginning of the Act, as the reader cannot understand the Act till he is master of the definitions or explanations of the terms used in the Act. Politically, their proper place is at the end of the Act, as a definition frequently narrows or widens the whole scope of an Act, and Parliament cannot possibly judge whether such narrowing or widening is or is not expedient till they are acquainted with the Act itself, *e.g.*, in the Contagious Diseases (Animals) Act, 1869, the definition, as it is called, of local authorities in the schedule determines the persons by whom, the places in which, and the funds out of which, the whole Act is to be carried into operation. This logical and political antagonism of arrangement might easily be reconciled were it the custom of Parliament to postpone the above sections in the same way as they postpone the preamble till the Bill has been gone through. Such a postponement, however, would, in a hardly fought Bill, give rise to a division. The draftsman, therefore, is recommended as a general rule to adhere to the political and not to the logical rule, and to place the sections in question at the end of the Act.

As to adjustment of existing and new law.—One of the most responsible duties of a draftsman is to provide for the adjustment of the provisions of the new Act which he is drawing, and the former law.

38. Adjustment of existing and new law.

Take a very simple case, the New Forest Act, 1877. The instructions to the draftsman would be to amend the constitution of the Court of Verderers by increasing the number of verderers to seven, one of whom should be nominated by the Crown, and the others be elected, the elective verderers to be chosen by the Parliamentary electors of the parishes and townships within the confines of the Forest, and by the commoners. The principles of this instruction are carried into effect by ss. 14–23, defining the constitution of the verderers, the qualification of the electors, the time at which the verderers come into office and their legal status. The details of their election are contained in Schedules 2 and 3, providing for a register of commoners and the mode of election of the verderers.

40 & 41 Vict. c. cxxi. (local.)

An examination of these clauses will show the necessity for the draftsman filling in the details of an instruction by sections which, though in one sense formal, in another require to be settled with great consideration. The draftsman must carefully look forward and see that the new body will be brought into action at the time fixed for the determination of the old body, and that there is no hiatus between the old and the new administration.

Frequently, however, more complicated cases arise in which provisions have to be inserted for abolishing an old authority and constituting a new one. Take for example the Bankruptcy Act, 1869, of which an analysis is found in Appendix (1). In that case, the instructions were to constitute a new London Bankruptcy Court, with a Chief Judge in Bankruptcy, and to abolish the Com missioners of the London Bankruptcy Court, and the country District Courts of Bankruptcy. The sections carrying into effect these purposes are arranged in Part VIII. under "Temporary provisions." The main objects of such sections are to transfer the officers of the existing London Court to the new court, and to compensate the officers of the abolished court. For the purpose of compensation the draftsman must acquaint himself with the rules of the Treasury and with the Superannuation Acts.

32 & 33 Vict. c. 71.

Another case may be cited, the Supreme Court of Judicature Act, 1873, in which the greater portion of the Act is occupied in the transfer of jurisdiction of the existing courts and the existing officers, and the declaration of the status of the existing officers when so transferred.

36 & 37 Vict. c. 66.

Where a new law is laid down establishing penalties on new manufactures, or bringing established manufactures within the

39. Exemptions and savings.

jurisdiction of an administrative body, a separate heading of exemptions and savings will usually be required. An illustration of this necessity will be found in the Explosives Act, 1875. These sections provide, amongst other things, for the exemption of Government factories, for cases of emergency in which a master of a ship or carrier transgresses the law by stress of weather or inevitable accident, and further, reserves in ss. 102–3. the common law liabilities in respect of nuisances and the powers of local Acts. Provisions such as these must always be kept in mind by the draftsman, and should be inserted by him when necessary without special instructions.

The section which most frequently raises the question of savings, is that of the repeal of Acts. As a general rule, when Acts are repealed, existing appointments and existing rights or privileges are maintained, and offences committed under the old Acts are punished in pursuance of the old provisions. Frequently, however, the draftsman will have to deviate from the above-mentioned rule. He will be required to abolish the old officers instead of retaining them, or to declare that the procedure of the new Acts is to be substituted in relation to the punishment of offences committed before the Act for the procedure under the old Acts and so forth. In short, he must be prepared to reconcile the provisions of the old and the new law by the insertion of such provisions as his legal knowledge will show him to be necessary for the proper working of the law.

It may be well to suggest here a provision which is often forgotten, viz., that in drawing a temporary Act which is to expire on a given day, and which imposes penalties or creates obligations, care must be taken to provide that offences committed and obligations incurred before the day appointed for its expiration may be punished or enforced after that day, or else the law will, in a great degree, fail of its purpose.

40. As to Schedules.

As to Schedules.—Great care should be taken in the preparation of schedules. It is desirable to include in a schedule matters of detail; it is improper to put in a schedule matters of principle. The drawing the proper line of demarcation between the two classes of matters is often difficult. All that can be said is that nothing should be placed in a schedule to which the attention of Parliament should be particularly directed; for example, the *constitution* of an electoral or financial body of persons should be found in the body of the Act; but the mode of conducting the election of the electoral body, and the rules as to proceedings at meetings of the financial body, may not improperly be placed in a schedule.

(margin: 38 & 39 Vict. c. 17. ss. 97–103.)

As to Alterations.—Great care must be taken in noticing any consequential alterations that may be required in consequence of amendments made in the passage of an Act through Parliament.

For example, a schedule is taken out, and nothing is more common than to find that the omission is noticed in one section, but the number of the schedules is forgotten to be altered in another section, and hence the schedules are misnumbered, and most important sections fail of effect.

With a view to obviate this difficulty the draftsman should note in the margin of each schedule the sections in which it is mentioned, and should refer to that note in the event of an alteration being made in any of such sections.

Similarly with respect to dates; the alteration of a date in one section not unfrequently necessitates the alteration of a date in another. This is forgotten in the haste of passing the Act through committee, and unless the alteration is attended to by the draftsman, the Act fails of effect in some material provision.

APPENDIX. I.

PART I.

ANALYSIS OF BANKRUPTCY ACT, 1869, 32 & 33 Vict. c. 71.

Preliminary, ss. 1–5.

Heads.

The Law

Adjudication and vesting of property, Part I.
- Adjudication, ss. 6–13.
- Appointment of trustee, ss. 14–18.

Administration of property, Part II.
- General provisions affecting administration of property, ss. 19–21.
- Dealings with bankrupt's property, ss. 22–30.
- Payment of debts and distribution of assets, ss. 31–40.
- Dividends, 41–46.
- Close of bankruptcy, s. 47.
- Discharge of bankrupt, ss. 48–50.
- Release of trustee, ss. 51–53.
- Status of undischarged bankrupt, s. 54.
- Audit, ss. 55–58.

Note.—Sections 47–55 ought to have formed a third division, under a title such as "Termination of bankruptcy." The headings of this Act might be materially improved in expression.

Authority to administer the law.

Constitution and powers of court, Part III.
- Description of court, ss. 59–72.
- Orders and warrants of court, ss. 73–77.
- General rules, s. 78.
- Change of jurisdiction by Chancellor, s. 79.

Supplemental Provisions.

Part IV.
- As to proceedings, ss. 80–82.
- As to trustees and committee of inspection, ss. 83, 84.
- As to power over bankrupt, ss. 85, 86.
- As to property devolving on trustee, ss. 87–95.
- As to discovery of bankrupt's property, ss. 96–99.
- Joint and separate estates, ss. 100–105.
- Evidence, ss. 106–109.
- Miscellaneous, ss. 110–119.

Persons having privilege of Parliament.
- Part V. ss. 120–124.

Note.——This part should have been omitted, it forms more properly the subject of a separate Bill.

Referential Provisions.

Liquidation by arrangement. Composition with creditors.
- Part VI. s. 125. Regulations.
- Part VII. ss. 126, 127. Regulations.

D 2

PART II.

PROVISIONS ANCILLARY TO IMPROVEMENT SCHEME.

As to Local Authority.

1. *Medical Officer.*

2. *Local Inquiry.*

3. *Acquisition of Land.*

4. *Expenses.*

PART III.

GENERAL PROVISIONS.

APPENDIX II.

TABLE OF FORMS.

Preliminary.

1. Short title.
2. Extent of Act.
3. Commencement of Act.
4. Construction of Act and short title.

DEFINITIONS.

Local.

5. " Metropolis."
 " County."
 " Quarter sessions."
 " Borough."
 " Urban sanitary district " and " authority."
 " Rural sanitary district " and " authority."
 " Port sanitary authority " and " district."
 " Improvement Act district."
 " Local Government district."
 " Local board."
 " Union."
 " Guardians."
 " Common fund."
 " Poor-law parish."
 " Overseers."
 " Highway district."
 " Highway board."
 " Highway parish."
 " Parish for ecclesiastical purposes."
 " Chief officer of police."
 " Police district."

Colonial.

6. " British possession."
 " Governor."
 " Colony."
 " Governor."

General Definitions

7. " Secretary of State."
 " Person."
 " Treasury."
 " Existing."
 " Prescribed."

These forms are mere precedents, and not model general forms to be adopted in every Bill. The draftsman must consider in each case whether any particular form will suit the Bill which he is preparing.

DRAFT of a BILL for amending the LAW relating to

WHEREAS

Be it therefore enacted by the Queen's most Excellent Majesty, by and with the advice and consent of the Lords Spiritual and Temporal, and Commons, in this present Parliament assembled, and by the authority of the same, as follows :

Preliminary.

Short title.
1. This Act may be cited as " The Act, 18 ."

Extent of Act.
(a.)
2. This Act shall not extend to Scotland or Ireland. This Act shall extend to the Channel Islands and the Isle of Man.

Commencement of Act.
(b.)
3. This Act shall, *except as in this Act specially provided*, come into operation on and after the day of , which date is in this Act referred to as the commencement of this Act.

Construction of Act and short title.
4. This Act, so far as is consistent with the tenor thereof, shall be construed as one with the Act of the session of the . and years of the reign of Her present Majesty, chapter , intituled , and in this Act referred to as the principal Act ; and this Act and the principal Act may be cited together as the Acts, and this Act may be cited separately as the Act, 18 .

DEFINITIONS.

Local.

5. In this Act, unless the context otherwise requires—

Metropolis :"
The expression " The Metropolis " means all parishes and places in which the Metropolitan Board of Works have for the time being power to levy the consolidated rate : (c)

(a.) It is almost needless to remark that an Act should not be extended to the Channel Islands or the Isle of Man except for some special reason.

(b.) The following clause is often required to be inserted when the machinery of an Act has to be set in motion by a Secretary of State before the Act is brought into practical operation : — " At any time after the passing of this Act, any appointment, " regulation, or order may be made, any notice issued, form prescribed, or act done " which appears to a Secretary of State necessary or proper to be made, issued, " prescribed, or done with a view to bring this Act into operation at the date of the " commencement thereof." The clause should be inserted in its proper place, usually towards the end of the Act.

(c.) This definition includes the City of London.

The expression "county" does not include a county of a city or a county of a town, but includes any riding, division, parts, or liberty of a county having a separate court of quarter sessions :

The expression "quarter sessions" includes general sessions :

The expression "borough" means any place for the time being subject to the Act of the session of the fifth and sixth years of the reign of King William the Fourth, chapter seventy-six, intituled "An Act to provide for the Regulation of Municipal Corporations in England and Wales," and any Act amending the same :

The expressions "urban sanitary district" and "urban sanitary authority" mean respectively an urban sanitary district and an urban sanitary authority within the meaning of the Public Health Act, 1875 :

The expressions "rural sanitary district" and "rural sanitary authority" mean respectively a rural sanitary district and a rural sanitary authority within the meaning of the Public Health Act, 1875 :

The expression "port sanitary authority" means a port sanitary authority within the meaning of the Public Health Act, 1875 ; and the expression "port sanitary district" means the district within the jurisdiction of such port sanitary authority :

The expression "Improvement Act district" means any area subject to the jurisdiction of any commissioners, trustees, or other persons invested by any Local Act of Parliament with powers of town government and rating ; and the expression "Improvement Commissioners" means any such commissioners, trustees, or other persons :

The expression "Local Government district" means any area subject to the jurisdiction of a local board constituted in pursuance of the Local Government Acts as defined by the Public Health Act 1875, or in pursuance of the Public Health Act 1875 ; and the expression "local board" means any board so constituted :

The expression "union" means a union of parishes under a general or local Act with a separate board of guardians, and includes a parish for which there is a separate board of guardians :

The expression "guardians" means guardians appointed under the Poor Law Amendment Act 1834 and the Acts amending the same, and includes guardians or other body of persons performing under any Local Act the like functions as guardians under the Poor Law Amendment Act 1834 :

The expression "common fund" means in the case of a union under a Local Act, and of a parish with a separate board of guardians the fund applicable to the relief of the poor of such union or parish :

The expression "parish" means any place for which a separate poor rate is or can be made, or for which a separate overseer is or can be appointed : (a.)

A.D. 1878.

"County :"
"Quarter sessions :"
"Borough :"
"Urban sanitary district" and "authority:"
38 & 39 Vict. c. 55.
"Rural sanitary district" and "authority :"
38 & 39 Vict. c. 55.
"Port sanitary authority" and "district:"
38 & 39 Vict. c. 55.
"Improvement Act Commissioners" and "district :"
"Local Government district :"
"Local board :"
38 & 39 Vict. c. 55.
"Union :"
"Guardians :"
4 & 5 Will. 4. c. 76.
"Common fund :"
"Poor law parish :"

(a.) In all Acts, unless there is something in the context inconsistent therewith, "parish" (among other meanings applicable to it) signifies a place for which a separate poor rate is or can be made, or for which a separate overseer is or can be appointed

" Overseers :"
" Highway
district :"
27 & 28 Vict.
c. 101. s. 1.

The expression "overseers" includes any person or body of persons performing the duties of overseers so far as regards the assessment, making, and collection of rates for the relief of the poor :

The expression "highway district" means a district formed in pursuance of the Highway Acts, and the Acts amending the same :

" Highway
board :"
27 & 28 Vict.
c. 101. s. 1.

The expression "highway board" means a highway board constituted in pursuance of the Highway Acts :

" Highway
parish :"

The expression "highway parish" means a place which separately maintains its own highways :

" Parish for
ecclesiastical
purposes :"

The expression "parish" means a parish, new parish, district, chapelry, or place within the limits of which a minister has an exclusive cure of souls :

" Chief officer
of police."

The expression "chief officer of police" means—

(1.) In the city of London and the liberties thereof, the Commissioner of City Police ; and

(2.) In the metropolitan police district, the Commissioner or any Assistant Commissioner of Metropolitan Police ; and

(3.) Elsewhere the chief constable, or head constable, or other officer, by whatever name called, having the chief command of the police in the police district in reference to which such expression occurs.

" Police
district."

The expression "police district" means—

(1.) The city of London and the liberties thereof ; and

(2.) The metropolitan police district ; and

(3.) Any area maintaining a separate police force, whether county, riding, division, liberty of a county, borough, town, union, or combination of places or place ; and all the police under one chief constable shall be deemed to constitute one force for the purposes of this section.

Colonial.

6. In this Act, unless the context otherwise requires—

" British pos-
session :"

The expression "British possession" means any part of Her Majesty's dominions exclusive of the United Kingdom.

All territories and places within Her Majesty's dominions which are under one legislature shall be deemed for the purposes of this Act to constitute one British possession ; and for the purposes of this definition, where there are local legislatures as well as a central legislature, the expression "legislature" means the central legislature only ; and

" Governor :"

The expression "governor" means the officer for the time being administering the government of a British possession.

" Colony :"

The expression "colony" means any part of Her Majesty's dominions exclusive of the United Kingdom, of the Channel Islands, of the Isle of Man, and of India. (*a.*)

(29 & 30 Vict. c. 113. s. 18). Consequently where the poor law parish alone is meant it is not absolutely necessary to define it. The definition includes a township having a separate poor rate.

(*a.*) As to the meaning of India, see 21 & 22 Vict. c. 106. s. 1. As respects

All territories and places within Her Majesty's dominions which are *A.D. 1878.*
under one legislature shall be deemed for the purposes of this Act
to constitute one colony ; and for the purposes of this definition,
where there are local legislatures as well as a central legislature the
expression " legislature " means the central legislature only ; and
The expression " governor " means the officer for the time being ad- " Governor."
ministering the government of a colony.

General Definitions.

7. In this Act, unless the context otherwise requires—
The expression " Secretary of State " means one of Her Majesty's "Secretary of State :"
Principal Secretaries of State :
The expression "the Treasury " means the Commissioners of Her " Treasury :"
Majesty's Treasury :
The expression "person " includes a body of persons corporate or " Person :"
unincorporate :
The expression "existing" means existing at the passing of this " Existing :"
Act :
The expression "prescribed " means prescribed by any rules [*or order* " Prescribed :"
or as the case may be], made in pursuance of this Act :
The expression "prescribed " means prescribed by any Act passed
either before or after the passing of this Act authorising, &c.

Orders and Rules.

8. Her Majesty may from time to time by Order in Council [*or* the Power of Her
Secretary of State may by order] make, and when made, revoke, add to, make Orders in
and alter, rules in relation to the following matters, or any of them [*or* Council.
for all or any of the following purposes]; (that is to say,)
  (1.)
  (2.)
  (3.)
  (4.)
An Order purporting to be made in pursuance of this section shall be
laid as soon as practicable before both Houses of Parliament, if Parliament be in session at the time of the making thereof, or if not, then as
soon as practicable after the beginning of the then next session of
Parliament.
CLAUSE A.—Provided, that if either House of Parliament resolve
within the next forty days after any such order has been laid before such
House, that such order or any part thereof, ought not to continue in force,
the order or part thereof in respect of which such resolution has been
passed shall, after the date of such resolution, cease to be of any force,
without prejudice, nevertheless, to the making of any other order in its
place, or to anything done in pursuance of any such order or part
thereof before the date of such resolution.

India, it may, in some cases, be necessary to define " Governor " to mean either the
Governor-General, or the Governor of any Presidency.

A.D. 1878.

CLAUSE B.—An order under this section shall not come into force until it has lain for forty days before both Houses of Parliament during the session of Parliament.

CLAUSE C.—An order under this section shall be published in the London Gazette, and shall come into operation at the date of the publication thereof in that Gazette, or at any later period mentioned in the order. (a.)

Evidence.

Evidence of register.

9. A register purporting to be kept in pursuance of this Act shall be deemed to be in the proper custody when in the custody of the registrar, and shall be of such a public nature as to be admissible on its mere production from that custody as evidence of all matters entered therein in pursuance of this Act. (b.)

Gazette to be evidence.

10. The publication in the London Gazette of any order made [by a Secretary of State] in pursuance of this Act, shall be evidence that such order was made and came into operation in manner provided by this Act. (c.)

Proving list, &c. by certified copy.

11. A list, or document, or order made by a local authority under this Act, may be proved by the production of a copy thereof, purporting to be certified to be a true copy by the clerk of the local authority.

Inspection of documents.

12. Any member of a local authority, without payment, and any ratepayer [or other person interested], upon payment of a fee not exceeding one shilling, may at any reasonable time during the hours of business inspect the minute books and documents in the possession or under the

---

(a.) Clause 8, with the subordinate clauses A, B, and C, provide for the following cases:—Clause 8 where an order is simply laid before Parliament. Clause A. will be added to Clause 8 where it is intended that an order should come into operation immediately, but should be subject to be annulled by a subsequent resolution of either House. Clause B. will be added to Clause 8 where it is intended that an order is to lie before Parliament for a certain period before it can take effect, and then takes effect without anything further. Clause C. may be added where it is intended that an order should come into operation on its publication in the London Gazette.

It is not usual to confer on Parliament a power of annulling an Order in Council. Where it is intended virtually to confer on Parliament such a power, the Bill should provide, not that the *order* should be submitted to Parliament, but that the *draft* order or scheme to be confirmed by the order should be submitted to Parliament with a power for Parliament to annul the same before it is presented to Her Majesty in Council.

(b.) By 14 & 15 Vict. c. 99. s. 14. it is provided that whenever any book or document is of such a public nature as to be admissible in evidence on its mere production from the proper custody, an examined copy or extract is admissible in evidence; also a copy or extract purporting to be certified to be a true copy or extract by the officer having the custody of the original; the officer is required to furnish such certified copy or extract, and penalties are imposed for falsification and forgery.

(c.) The Documentary Evidence Act, 1868, provides for evidence of the contents of orders made by government departments, but where subsequent conditions are required before such order comes into operation, e.g., the having lain before Parliament or otherwise, some clause should be inserted making the production of some easily accessible document primâ facie evidence of the performance of the conditions of the Act.

control of the local authority, and shall be entitled to obtain copies and extracts therefrom on payment of such fee not exceeding   , as may from time to time be fixed by the local authority.

Any person who, having the custody of any such books or documents as aforesaid,—

(1.) Obstructs any person authorised to inspect the same in making such inspection thereof as in this section mentioned ; or,

(2.) Refuses to give copies or extracts to any person entitled to obtain the same under this section ;

shall, on summary conviction, be liable to a fine not exceeding two pounds.

Byelaws.

13. The local authority may from time to time, make, and when made, alter, add to, and repeal byelaws for all or any of the following purposes ; that is to say,

(1.)
(2.)
(3.)

Fines may be imposed for the breach of any such byelaws, provided that no fine exceeds for any one offence the sum of two pounds, or in the case of a continuing offence the sum of one pound for every day during which such offence is continued.

Power of local authority to make and alter byelaws.

A byelaw made in pursuance of this section, and any alteration in, addition to, and repeal of a byelaw shall not be of any validity until it has been confirmed by a Secretary of State [*or* Local Government Board].

A byelaw made under this Act shall not, nor shall any alteration in, or addition to, or repeal of a byelaw, be confirmed as aforesaid until the expiration of at least one month after notice of the intention to apply for confirmation of the same has been given by the local authority in some newspaper or newspapers circulating within the district to which the byelaws relate.

During the month next preceding the application for confirmation as aforesaid the local authority shall cause a printed copy of any byelaw, or alteration in, addition to, or repeal of a byelaw to be kept at their office in such manner as to be open during office hours to the inspection of all persons interested without fee, and shall also supply printed copies of such byelaw, alteration in, addition to, or repeal of a byelaw to any applicant on payment of a sum not exceeding sixpence for each copy.

The local authority shall supply copies of all byelaws made under this section and for the time being in force, to any applicant on payment of a sum not exceeding sixpence for each copy.

The production of a copy of any byelaw purporting to be certified by the clerk of the local authority to be a true copy of a byelaw for the time being in force, shall be evidence of such byelaw and of the due making and confirmation of such byelaw and of its being in force.

All fines imposed by a byelaw under this Act may be recovered on summary conviction.

Purchase of Lands by Local Authority.

A.D. 1878.

Power to purchase lands.

Incorporation of Lands Clauses Acts excluding the compulsory powers.
8 & 9 Vict. c. 18.
23 & 24 Vict. c. 106.
32 & 33 Vict. c. 18.

Incorporation of Lands Clauses Act allowing exercise of compulsory powers by provisional order.
8 & 9 Vict. c. 18.
23 & 24 Vict. c. 106.
32 & 33 Vict. c. 18.

Compulsory purchase of land by provisional order.

14. A local authority may purchase such lands as they may require for the purposes of this Act, subject to the regulations in this Act contained.

15.* With a view to the purchase of lands for the purposes of this Act, the Lands Clauses Consolidation Acts 1845 1860 and 1869, shall be incorporated with this Act, with the exception of the provisions of the Lands Clauses Consolidation Act 1845, which relate to the purchase and taking of lands otherwise than by agreement, and to the sale of superfluous land, and to access to the special Act. In construing the said Lands Clauses Consolidation Acts for the purposes of this Act, this Act shall be deemed to be the special Act, and the local authority shall be deemed to be the promoters of the undertaking.

16. With a view to the purchase of lands for the purposes of this Act, the Lands Clauses Consolidation Acts 1845 1860 and 1869, shall be incorporated with this Act, with the exception of the provisions of the Lands Clauses Consolidation Act 1845 which relate to the sale of superfluous land and to access to the special Act. In construing the said Lands Clauses Consolidation Acts for the purposes of this Act this Act shall be deemed to be the special Act, and the local authority shall be deemed to be the promoters of the undertaking; [but the provisions of the said Lands Clauses Consolidation Acts which relate to the purchase and taking of lands otherwise than by agreement shall not be put into operation except in accordance with the regulations in this Act in that behalf mentioned].

17. With respect to the purchase and taking of lands otherwise than by agreement the following regulations shall have effect:

(1.) The local authority shall publish once at the least in each of three consecutive weeks in the month of September or October, or November, in some one and the same newspaper circulating within the jurisdiction of the local authority, an advertisement describing shortly the objects for which the lands are proposed to be taken, naming a place within or near the district of the local authority where a plan of the lands proposed to be taken may be seen at all reasonable hours, and stating the quantity of such lands.

* Clauses 15, 16, and 17 relate to the incorporation of the Lands Clauses Consolidation Acts. Clause 15 empowers a local authority to purchase land by agreement, and may be inserted in any Act in which a local authority desires to purchase land for public purposes. Clauses 16 and 17 provide for cases where the local authority have an obligation thrown upon them to perform a duty which cannot be performed without the purchase of land, and enable that authority to enforce the compulsory clauses of the Lands Clauses Consolidation Act with the assent of Parliament obtained through the intervention of the Local Government Board. If the words enclosed in brackets in Clause 16 are omitted, that clause clothes the local authority with an absolute power of purchasing lands compulsorily at any time within three years after the passing of the Act. Such a clause must never be inserted except under special instructions, and in respect of lands specifically described or referred to in the Act itself.

A.D. 1878.

(2.) During the month next following the month in which such advertisements are published, the local authority shall serve a notice on every owner or reputed owner, lessee or reputed lessee, and occupier of the lands proposed to be taken, so far as such persons can be reasonably ascertained, describing the lands proposed to be taken from the person so served, and requiring an answer stating whether he assents, dissents, or is neuter in respect of the taking of such lands :

Where any person above-mentioned as required to be served is absent abroad or cannot be found, notice may be served on his agent, or if no agent can be found, may be served by leaving the same on the premises :

Service of a notice on a person, whether principal or agent, may be made in any of the following methods, by delivery of the same personally, or by leaving the same at the usual or last known place of abode of the principal or agent, or by forwarding the same by post in a prepaid letter addressed to the usual or last known place of abode of such principal or agent :

One notice addressed to the occupier or occupiers of a house without naming him or them, and left at that house, shall be deemed to be a notice served on the occupier or on all the occupiers of that house :

Any notice required to be served on a number of persons having any right or interest in common in or over lands, shall be sufficient if served on any three or more of such persons :

Where a notice is served by post it shall be deemed to have been served at the time when the letter containing the same would be delivered in the ordinary course of post, and in proving such service it shall be sufficient to prove that the letter containing the notice was properly addressed and put into the post :

(3.) On compliance with the provisions of this section with respect to advertisements and notices, the local authority may, if they think fit, present a petition under their seal to the [Local Government Board] in respect of the whole or any part of the lands included in their notices. The petition shall state the objects for which the lands are proposed to be taken, and the quantity of lands proposed to be taken, with a short description thereof, and the names of the owners or reputed owners, lessees or reputed lessees, and occupiers of lands, who have assented dissented or are neuter in respect of the taking of such lands, or who have returned no answer to the notice ; it shall pray that the local authority, with reference to the lands proposed in the petition to be taken may be allowed to put in force the powers of the said Lands Clauses Consolidation Acts with respect to the purchase and taking of lands otherwise than by agreement, and the prayer shall be supported by such evidence as the [Local Government Board] requires :

(4.) If on the consideration of the petition and on proof of the proper advertisements having been published and notices served [the Local Government Board] think fit to proceed with the case, they shall cause such inquiry as they think necessary to be made either in the district in which the lands are situate or otherwise respecting the propriety of assenting to the prayer of such petition :

(5.) After receiving the report made upon such inquiry [the Local Government Board] may make a provisional order, empowering the local authority to put in force, with reference to the lands referred to in the petition or any of such lands, the powers of the said Lands Clauses Consolidation Acts with respect to the purchase and taking of lands otherwise than by agreement, and that either absolutely or with such conditions and modifications as the Board may think fit, and it shall be the duty of the local authority to serve a copy of the provisional order so made on the persons and in the manner on whom and in which notices in respect of the lands referred to in the order are required by this Act to be served, except tenants for a month or a less period than a month :

(6.) A provisional order made in pursuance of this section shall not be of any validity until and unless it has been confirmed by Act of Parliament, and it shall be lawful for the [Local Government Board], as soon as conveniently may be, to obtain such confirmation. If, while the Bill confirming any such order is pending in either House of Parliament, a petition is presented against such order, the Bill, so far as it relates to such order, may be referred to a Select Committee, and the petitioner shall be allowed to appear and oppose as in the case of private Bills :

(7.) A provisional order made in pursuance of this Act, when confirmed by Parliament, with such modifications, if any, as may seem fit to Parliament, shall have full effect, and the Act confirming the same shall be deemed to be a Public General Act.

Order as to costs.

18. The [Local Government Board] may, if they think fit, make such order as they think just in favour of any person whose lands have been proposed to be taken compulsorily for the allowance of the reasonable costs, charges, and expenses properly incurred by him in opposing the taking of such lands.

The costs, charges, and expenses allowed by such order (if any) and all costs, charges, and expenses incurred by the [Local Government Board] in relation to any provisional order under this Act shall, to such amount as the [Board] think proper to direct, be deemed to be an expense incurred by the local authority under this Act, and shall be paid to such person and to the [Local Government Board] respectively, in such manner, and at such times, and either in one sum or by instalments, as the [Local Government Board] may order, with power for the [Local Government Board] to direct interest to be paid at such rate, not ex-

A.D. 1878.

ceeding five pounds in the hundred by the year, as the [Local Government Board] may determine, upon any sum for the time being due in respect of such costs, charges, and expenses as aforesaid.

An order made by the [Local Government Board] in pursuance of this section may be made a rule of the High Court of Justice, and be enforced accordingly.

Power of Local Authority to borrow.

19. The local authority may from time to time, in manner provided by the Local Loans Act, 1875, and subject to the provisions thereof, borrow at interest, on the security of the [local rate] such moneys as they from time to time think requisite for the purposes of this Act not exceeding the sum of   .

The whole of the money borrowed under this Act, whether as one loan or as several loans, shall be discharged within a period not exceeding   years from the   day of   [or from the date of the first advance of money made on account of any loan under this Act].

The local authority may raise such loan, or any part thereof, by the issue of debenture stock. (*a.*)

Power to local authority to borrow on rate. 38 & 39 Vict. c. 83.

20. Where a loan by a local authority, or any part thereof, is discharged by an annual appropriation of a fixed sum, the local authority shall, until such loan or part of a loan is discharged, within twenty-one days after the expiration of each year, transmit to the Local Government Board a return in such form and verified in such manner as the Board from time to time direct, showing the amount which has been raised and appropriated for the purpose of the said annual appropriation during the year next preceding the making of such return, and the manner in which the same has been appropriated, and the total amount (if any) of the sum raised remaining unappropriated at the end of the year. If it appears to the Local Government Board by such return or otherwise that the local authority have failed to comply with the provisions of the Local Loans Act, 1875, or this Act, with respect to the raising or appropriation of the said fixed sum, that Board may, if they think fit, and after hearing the local authority, if desirous of being heard, by order direct that the sum in respect of which default has been made is to be raised and applied according to law ; and such order may be enforced by mandamus.

Supervision of Local Government Board in case of annual appropriation.

38 & 39 Vict. c. 83.

Legal Proceedings.

21. All offences and fines under this Act, the prosecution or recovery of which is not otherwise provided for by this Act, may be prosecuted and recovered in manner provided by the Summary Jurisdiction Act, and all money and costs directed by this Act to be recovered in a sum-

Prosecution of offences.

(*a.*) Under s. 6. debenture stock can only be issued by a local authority expressly authorised. This authority should not be given as a matter of course, or where the amount is small.

mary manner may be recovered on complaint in manner provided by the said Act.

For the purposes of this section the expression " Summary Jurisdiction Act," means the Act of the session of the eleventh and twelfth years of the reign of Her present Majesty, chapter forty-three, intituled "An Act to facilitate the performance of the duties of justices of the " peace out of sessions within England and Wales with respect to " summary convictions and orders," inclusive of any Acts amending the same. (*a.*)

Summary proceedings.

22. Any dispute or matter in respect of which jurisdiction is given by this Act to a court of summary jurisdiction shall be deemed to be a matter on which that court has authority by law to make an order on complaint in pursuance of the Summary Jurisdiction Act. (*b.*)

Notices.

Notices, &c. may be printed or written.

23. Notices, orders, and other documents under this Act may be in writing or print, or partly in writing and partly in print; and where any notice, order, or document requires authentication by the local authority the signature thereof by the clerk to the local authority shall be sufficient authentication.

Service of notices.

24. Any notice, order, or document required or authorised by this Act to be served on any person may be served—

(*a.*) By delivering the same to such person ; or

(*b.*) By leaving the same at the usual or last known place of abode of such person ; or

(*c.*) By forwarding the same by post in a prepaid letter addressed to such person at his usual or last known place of abode.

If the notice is served by post it shall be deemed to have been served at the time when the letter containing the notice would be delivered in the ordinary course of post, and in proving such service it shall be sufficient to prove that the letter containing the notice was properly addressed and put into the post.

A notice, order, or document by this Act required or authorised to be served on the owner or occupier of any premises, shall be deemed to be properly addressed if addressed by the description of the " owner " or " occupier " of the premises (naming them), without further name or description.

A notice, order, or document by this Act required or authorised to be served on the owner or occupier of premises may be served by delivering the same, or a true copy thereof, to some person on the premises, or if there is no person on the premises to whom the same

---

(*a.*) This definition of Summary Jurisdiction Act will be inserted in the definitions when the expression is used in any other part of the Bill besides this clause.

(*b.*) This clause is drawn to accord with the language of section 1 of 11 & 12 Vict. c. 43., which applies where a court of summary jurisdiction has power to make an order on complaint.

can with reasonable diligence be delivered, by fixing the notice on some conspicuous part of the premises. A.D. 1878.

Saving Clauses.

25. Where in any place to which this Act applies any local Act is in force providing for objects the same as or similar to the objects of this Act, the enactments of such local Act may be enforced at the discretion of the local authority either instead of or in concurrence with this Act; provided that— *Relation of local Acts to general Acts.*

(1.) The local authority of any place to which this Act applies shall not by reason of any local Act within its jurisdiction be exempted 'from the performance of any duty or obligation to which such authority are subject under this Act; and that

(2.) A person shall not be punished twice for the same offence.

26. This Act shall not exempt any person from any proceeding for an offence which is punishable at common law, or under any Act of Parliament other than this Act, so that a person be not punished twice for the same offence. *Saving clause as to liability to other criminal proceedings.*

When proceedings are taken before a court against a person in respect of an offence under this Act, which is also an offence punishable with some higher punishment either at common law or under some Act of Parliament other than this Act, the court may direct that, instead of such proceedings being continued, proceedings shall be taken for punishing such person with such higher punishment at common law or under some Act of Parliament other than this Act.

27. All powers given by this Act shall be deemed to be in addition to and not in derogation of any other powers conferred on any local authority by Act of Parliament, and the local authority may exercise any such powers in the same manner as if this Act had not passed. *Powers of Act cumulative.*

28. The institution of any criminal proceeding against or the conviction of any person for any act made an offence by this Act shall not affect any remedy which any other person aggrieved by such act may be entitled to in any civil proceeding. *Saving of civil remedy.*

29. Nothing in this Act shall entitle any person to refuse to make a complete discovery in any legal proceeding, or to answer any question or interrogatory in a civil proceeding, in any court; but such discovery or answer shall not be admissible in evidence against such person in any criminal proceeding under this or any other Act of Parliament. *Saving of obligation to make discovery.*

Repeal. (a.)

30. The Acts specified in the   schedule to this Act are hereby repealed, from and after the commencement of this Act, to the extent specified in the third column of that schedule. *Repeal of Acts in schedule.*

(a.) This clause will probably never be required to be inserted in its entirety. It is intended to convey suggestions as to numerous savings, some one or more of which is or are frequently required to be inserted. Still further savings will be found in the Statute Law Revision Acts, 1863, 1867, and 1870–1876.

Provided that—

(1.) Any Order in Council or warrant made, and any license or certificate granted under any enactment hereby repealed, shall continue in force as if it had been made or granted under this Act; and

(2.) Any enactment or document referring to any Act or enactment hereby repealed shall be construed to refer to this Act, or to the corresponding enactment in this Act:

(3.) This repeal shall not affect—

(a.) The past operation of any enactment hereby repealed, nor anything duly done or suffered under any enactment hereby repealed ; nor

(b.) Any right, privilege, obligation, or liability acquired, accrued, or incurred under any enactment hereby repealed ; nor

(c.) Any penalty, forfeiture, or punishment incurred in respect of any offence committed against any enactment hereby repealed ; nor

(d.) Any investigation, legal proceeding, or remedy in respect of any such right, privilege, obligation, liability, penalty, forfeiture, or punishment as aforesaid; and any such investigation, legal proceeding, and remedy may be carried on as if this Act had not passed ; and

(4.) This repeal shall not revive any enactment, right, office, privilege, matter, or thing not in force or existing at the commencement of this Act.

INDEX.

A.

B.

C.

G.

H.

I.

L.

LONDON:
Printed by GEORGE E. EYRE and WILLIAM SPOTTISWOODE,
Printers to the Queen's most Excellent Majesty.
For Her Majesty's Stationery Office.
[B 591.—250.—8/78.]

www.ingramcontent.com/pod-product-compliance
Lightning Source LLC
Chambersburg PA
CBHW021528270326
41930CB00008B/1145